Gareth Jones

On Assignment in Nazi Germany 1933-34

Ray Gamache

welsh academic press

Cardiff

Published in Wales by Welsh Academic Press, an imprint of

Ashley Drake Publishing Ltd
PO Box 733
Cardiff
CF14 7ZY

www.welsh-academic-press.wales

First Impression – 2021
Revised Edition – 2022

978-1-86057-148-0 (paperback)
978-1-86057-153-4 (eBook)

British Library Cataloguing-in-Publication Data.
A CIP catalogue for this book is available from the British Library.

Typeset by Prepress Plus, India (www.prepressplus.in)
Cover design by Welsh Books Council, Aberystwyth, Wales

Contents

To
Rachel J. (Dube) Gamache, 1922-2021

Author's Note

I have attempted to make the text as readable as possible, given the differences in spelling, capitalization, and punctuation from the 1930s to the present. Transcriptions of the pocket diary notebooks used for the articles under consideration are my own, other than passages in Welsh and German, for which I sought assistance.

Nigel Colley and I had co-transcribed the 1933 and 1931 diary notebooks used for Jones's journeys to the Soviet Union, with considerable assistance from Naomi Field, Alan Richards, and Wynford Jones, and those have been used in this study where applicable.

The National Library of Wales has made digital versions of most all personal correspondence and a large trove of the pocket diary notebooks and the pocket appointment diaries available through their website. In this study, I show correspondence between pocket diary notebooks and the newspaper articles stemming from his travels to and reporting on Germany, and I have attempted to account for what I perceive to be discrepancies in descriptions and cataloguing.

The information contained in those notebooks constitute much of the raw material found in Jones's newspaper articles and a good deal more as well. Using the appointment diaries is a necessary component in tracking Jones's meetings, engagements, and interviews. I would, however, not claim that this study is comprehensive, even given its limited focus on Germany.

The number of people with whom Jones interacted and documented is large, compacted into a relatively short time period. In selecting which people to include, the author has assembled a cast whose experiences are brought to bear in this representation. I make no claim to infallibility; however, I stand behind my argument as articulated, and I certainly hope the next generation of scholars will correct obvious flaws and errors.

Acknowledgements

This book began as a proposal for the German-Ukrainian Historical Commission conference scheduled for September 2020 but canceled due to Covid-19. As soon as the proposal had been submitted in late April, I realized I had enough material to attempt a monograph and perhaps even a book.

Working from the list of articles at the garethjones.org website compiled by Dr. Alun Jones, I used the British Newspaper Archive to add a few more newspaper articles by Jones to that list, as well as several stories covering speeches, debates, and presentations in which Jones was the subject. Adverts published in the *Western Mail* about different series Jones produced are also mentioned.

Some of the Gareth Jones archival material has been digitized and made available at the National Library of Wales in Aberystwyth. Archival material belonging to private individuals who have shared with me parts of their collections was also used. Russ Chelak was instrumental in making some of the first digital images of the pocket notebook diaries and letters.

This project was greatly helped by two webinars – one by Rob Phillips of the National Library of Wales on the Jones archive and another hosted by Pascal Trees for the German-Ukrainian Historical Commission. I wish to extend my appreciation for their assistance in this endeavor.

I also wish to thank those people at the University of Chicago Library and Cambridge University for assistance in tracking down archival material included in this work. Thanks especially to Angela Jackson, who provided the photograph of the Stewarts from Frida Stewart's memoir, *Firing a Shot for Freedom*, and to Simon Deefholts at the Clapton Press for putting me in touch with Ms. Jackson. I also wish to thank Samara Pearce for access to the photographs of Alexander Wienerberger.

Acknowledgements

I also wish to thank the two people who read an early draft of the book and who provided needed advice and suggestions on how to improve it, namely, Wynford Jones and Jane Margaret Benesch. I also want to thank those non-readers who endured my digressions about the work in progress, Kathy and John Leggett, Diane and Paul Visich, and Sarah Benesch, with whom I enjoyed summer boat beers, as well as Amy Benesch for her much needed tennis prognostications during the French Open.

Finally, given the presence of the virus, this was very much a home-grown affair. What I have been able to accomplish is due to the loving affection of Jane, Sammie, and Dargan, without whose calm presence I could not thrive. Living through this worldwide pandemic that has claimed so many lives and brought pain and suffering to so many more makes me appreciate how every moment is precious.

"But scholarship without courage is not worth the paper it is printed on."

Henry R. Huttenbach

"Whether or not this was intended, moral commitments of historians, and other scholars for that matter, need to be made explicit and supported by evidence open to scrutiny. Historians, by professional obligation, must also be willing to put forward arguments about their commitments and values rather than just asserting them, as well as explain openly, to a wider public, the processes through which judgements are reached."

Johan Öhman

"Only the fearful imagination of those who have been aroused by such reports but have not actually been smitten in their own flesh, of those who are consequently free from the bestial, desperate terror which, when confronted by real, present horror, inexorably paralyzes everything that is not mere reaction, can afford to keep thinking about horrors."

Hannah Arendt

"For even if the rational mind were not obstructed by the delusionary nature of the Nazi project, it would repeatedly be tempted to doubt its own sanity, haunted by visions of an alternative reality that would hardly exist on the Dog Star if it were suffering from rabies. Only in a febrile delirium could the fantasies of fascism acquire reality and its illusions be transformed into actions, which are then dissolved into hot air by a dissimulating machine which they call the Wolff Bureau. They manage – by a further projection – to find themselves encircled by a world of enemies who only want peace. This is the same pernicious vicious circle as before, one that inverts cause and effect, self-obsessed, never reflecting on what the world thinks of it."

Karl Kraus

1

So Sincere, Fair, and Sympathetic

'take the opposite view'

This study addresses the criticism that Gareth Jones was a Nazi sympathizer assisting the Third Reich's propaganda ministry to spread the "lie" that Ukrainian peasants were starving and that millions would die. Jones announced the dire conditions in Ukraine (the Ukrainian Soviet Socialist Republic - SSR) at a news conference on March 29, 1933, in Berlin, three days before the Nazis imposed a boycott of Jewish businesses throughout Germany. The implication is that Jones was strategic in deciding to make his famine announcement in Berlin, after having left Moscow on March 25, and then staying in Danzig with Reinhard Haferkorn, League of Nations high commissioner for Danzig, professor of classical literature, and future member of the Nazi propaganda ministry, to craft a lengthy letter to David Lloyd George outlining the situation confronting the Soviet Union.

The narrative of Jones being wittingly (or unwittingly) used to further Nazi ends is based on

Gareth Vaughan Jones, 1933.

I

the premise that Jones, in having created "an alternative news story to the foreign press to divert their eyes" from the boycott, "played right into the Nazis hands, demonizing the communists..."[1] The argument is corroborated by a letter Jones wrote to Haferkorn and Wilhelm Wiss, a Nazi propagandist, several months later, in which Jones disavowed the criticisms he had leveled against Adolph Hitler and the Nazi Party in a series of articles written the *Western Mail* in June 1933, following a visit to Germany.

> You should not take seriously what I said about Hitler and the Nazi movement. That's what I always do whenever I have a discussion with someone of strong opinions, I always take the opposite view so that the ideas will become clearer to me and the proponent will argue with greater conviction.[2]

This letter, written in response to German concerns that Jones had been overly critical, hardly serves as a persuasive confession, though Jones deftly rationalized how his newspaper articles might be read to show there was nothing particularly sinister in them. The idea that Jones was attempting to raise within readers a stronger argument to defend Hitler and his Aryan ideology loses credence when compared with the actual newspaper articles he had written in June 1933 during a tour to assess conditions, especially relating to the Jews after decrees like the Law for the Restoration of the Professional Civil Service were passed, barring Jews from practicing in most professions. Rather, Jones's letter may be read as an obvious deception to justify his having criticized Hitler and the Nazis but wanting

Gareth Jones with his friend Reinhard Haferkorn.

2

to maintain access. The same rationale could have been used after his February series as well. For example, when Jones wrote that the Nazi rally he attended in Frankfurt, "... is primitive, mass worship," and "The people are drunk with nationalism. It is hysteria..."[3] the reader is supposed to conclude that Jones was not criticizing Nazi ideology *per se*, because the hysteria it invoked was effectively steeling German peoples' resolve in support of Hitler.

Such an interpretation, bolstered with evidence that as a student he stereotyped Jews and failed to confront and condemn antisemitism when he experienced it, would be meaningful were it corroborated with textual evidence; otherwise, it is more reasonable to assume Jones was assuaging contacts in the German government that he thought best to placate. Historiography of news coverage of Hitler's rise to power confirms this unequivocally. For example, journalists like Rothay Reynolds, Sefton Delmer, Norman Ebbutt, and Edgar Ansel Mowrer all faced difficulties in how to characterize Nazi brutality and maintain access. Mowrer would be expelled. Jones used his contacts prudently, and the textual evidence reveals that he only became more scathing in his criticisms of Hitler and the Nazis.

The Wiss letter takes on ominous overtones when read in isolation, and out of context with everything else Jones wrote about Germany. When Jones died in 1935, memorializing his love of Germany in an obituary published in *Völkischer Beobachter* was relatively easy for Wiss, who enclosed a self-translated copy in a letter he sent to Jones's family. "No one else has ever been so sincere, fair, and sympathetic also with my country and the man all Germans love so much."[4] Again, the implication that Wiss made was shaped purposefully: Jones was beyond anyone else in his love for Germany and Hitler. The article that Wiss himself translated and enclosed with his letter to Jones's family after Gareth's death in 1935 should be seen for what it was – an appropriation of Jones's legacy for Nazi propaganda purposes, not for Jones himself, but for his articles revealing Soviet failures in agriculture with which German Marxists were demonized.

The argument that Jones's reporting of mass starvation in the Soviet Union cleverly served Nazi propaganda purposes is developed courtesy of Jones's known affinity for Germany and the German people; however, the underlying trope is that Jones's reporting was

3

meant to belittle the Soviet Union. It is a trope derived from the same logic employed in the publication of Walter Duranty's article, "Russians Hungry, But Not Starving," published by the *New York Times* on March 31, 1933, to deny that mass starvation was occurring in Ukraine and to denigrate Gareth Jones by name.[5]

'grim facts will out'

Denial of mass starvation in Ukraine throughout the summer and autumn of 1933 created a necessary diversion enabling the United States and the Soviet Union to conduct negotiations that ultimately led to the U.S.'s recognition of the Soviet Union on November 16, 1933.[6] The competing narratives about what happened in the winter of 1932-1933 were largely the result of contradictory newspaper articles. Jones himself recognized what forces were at play, when he wrote in early May 1933 a Letter to the Editor responding to Duranty's assertions. Jones conceded that Western journalists were working in the Soviet Union under strict censorship by the Foreign Press Department headed up by Konstantin Umansky. Jones was tactful in explaining that the Politburo's attempts to conceal the mass starvation by censoring foreign journalists had turned reporters like Duranty into "masters of euphemisms."

> The Soviet Government tries its best to conceal the situation, but the grim facts will out. Under the conditions of censorship existing in Moscow, foreign journalists have to tone down their messages and have become masters at the art of understatement. The existence of the general famine is none the less true, in spite of the fact that Moscow still has bread.[7]

Jones understood why Duranty and others were forced to "give 'famine' the polite name of 'food shortage' and 'starving to death' was sanitized to 'widespread mortality from diseases due to malnutrition.'"[8] That people in Ukraine, the North Caucasus, and the Lower Volga were starving to death Duranty labeled "a big scare story."

4

Rather than level accusations against fellow journalists working under duress, Jones delineated the causes for mass starvation, pointing to the policies of forced collectivization, the massacre of livestock, dekulakization, and the export of wheat. When Eugene Lyons, United Press correspondent stationed in Moscow, memorialized the entire affair in his 1937 memoir, *Assignment in Utopia*, Jones was portrayed as the victim. "Poor Gareth Jones must have been the most surprised human being alive when the facts he so painstakingly garnered from our mouths were snowed under by our denials."[9]

Despite both factual and analytical errors in Lyons's recounting, the myth of Jones being buried beneath an avalanche of denials, falsifications, and re-appropriations served to deflect criticism that Western journalists had not done enough to reveal the utter depravity of Stalinist terror. After Jones was murdered in 1935, he fell into total obscurity for almost 70 years. In that same time frame, Ukrainians struggled for recognition of the *Holodomor* as genocide. That struggle intensified when interest in Jones resurfaced with the publication of his biography in 2005 and a few years later with an exhibition at Cambridge University's Wren Library of his 1933 Soviet notebook-diaries. Jones became a central figure in Ukraine's historical culture because his reporting publicly gave voice to those Ukrainians who had perished from starvation. Jones had understood the event as a humanitarian crisis that needed to be addressed, as specified in the League of Nation's creation of the International Red Cross. He alerted the world to the "grim facts" of mass starvation that he accurately characterized as worse than the Volga Famine of 1920-21, and he worked with religious and pacifist groups to petition the Soviet Union to provide food to the hungry. Western governments' failure to confront Stalinist terror only legitimated its use by a dictator on innocent people. And in June 1933, shortly after Jones returned from the Soviet Union, Jones warned that Hitler and the Nazis were persecuting German Jews.

With the release of several documentary and fictionalized film accounts of his life over the past decade, Jones has become the iconic journalist of the *Holodomor*. Jones was neither the first nor the only Western journalist to write about mass starvation in Ukraine; in fact, Malcolm Muggeridge became the British journalist most often associated with famine reporting as he was featured in the

1986 television broadcast of *Harvest of Despair*, a documentary that followed publication of the Robert Conquest study, *Harvest of Sorrow*.

Jones's reemergence into public consciousness took on added significance when Jones was elevated to the status of "Hero of Ukraine." That a little-known foreign journalist should occupy such a position attests to the importance of his reporting. By keeping Ukrainian victims' experiences alive through the discursive act of writing newspaper articles that provided eyewitness testimony, Jones assured access to representations of what happened in a way that brought a personal scope to this catastrophic humanitarian tragedy.

Because Jones died before turning 30 and never had the opportunity to reflect on his own reporting about the *Holodomor* or the rise of Hitler's dictatorship, we are left with remnants that have been woven together to create a portrait of Jones that is as complicated as the historiography of the *Holodomor* and its use in shaping Ukrainian identity through historical culture.

Discourse, Media, and Context

Any investigative study of journalism history is actualized in the process of creating coherence from archival fragments. How researchers assemble a coherent image of a journalist from newspaper articles, notebooks, manuscripts, memorabilia, photographs, and personal correspondence arguably runs counter to what Lawrence Grossberg has characterized as the ontological turn.[10] In a post-truth, post-survivor world in which all competing narratives about historic events are equally relative, there is nothing but the texts, even though texts do not even really exist. Untethered from biography and context, information only exists for and of itself. The legacy of the last decades in literary studies has suggested any form of critique is symptomatic and a part of the very thing it is critiquing. Grossberg argues the way forward is partly avoiding relativism and certainty, partly not assuming that scholars know how people experience the world.

> I believe it is the task of critical work to make visible the relations that remain invisible or even refuse to appear, not because they are

necessarily hidden secrets nor because we are blind or stupid, but because we have not looked with other tools (concepts). It is the task of critical work first to separate and then to fuse a multiplicity of demands and powers, of failures and limits, into the possibility of finding the unity and commonality in the difference and multiplicity.[11]

The best way to show how Gareth Jones experienced the world is to make visible the stories, letters, and speeches he wrote, contextualized around those experiences dealing with Germany.

Anchored within the theoretical foundation of critical discourse and radical contextualization, this study is modeled on methodology suggested for the application of critical discourse analysis to media texts.[12] The framework calls for textual analysis that focuses attention on the practices and professional standards and constructs of a newspaper, its actors, objects, discursive strategies, and ideological standpoints.

Understanding journalism as a practice involves a theoretical and historical (re)-construction of its context. Additionally, the critical discourse analysis framework structures synchronic and diachronic analyses, meaning both comparative and longitudinal analyses are utilized. In this way, events and specific issues are associated to the broader issues under consideration. For example, analysis of Jones's series of newspaper articles covering Hitler's rise to power can be compared with his coverage of the Soviet Union, as they were designed as one series titled "A Welshman Looks at Europe." They should also be compared with other articles he wrote about Germany and the Soviet Union as well as compared with contemporaries' articles on the same issues. This serves as an exemplar of the importance of intertextuality, which not only delineates a text's relationship with other texts, but also involves the relationship between the social actors, their sources, and the texts they produce.[13] Lastly, this study adumbrates the conditions under which newspaper articles were constituted within the wider sphere of politics, economy, religion, and historical culture. Foreign correspondents stationed in Berlin often gathered at the *Taverne*, 134 Kurfürstenstrasse, an Italian restaurant in Berlin's center, where American, British, and French journalists kept a table reserved permanently, providing reporters with a safe haven from Nazi pressure.

While Jones remained, in his own words, a fervent Liberal and pacifist who preferred free trade, disarmament, and the League of Nations, he certainly held deeply rooted views about governments in the Soviet Union, Germany, France, Great Britain, and the United States. Apparent inconsistencies, revealed in personal correspondence and in newspaper articles, present researchers with opportunities to make assumptions about who Jones was and what Jones believed. Rather than allowing the texts to serve as the basis for his views and beliefs, it is easier to label Jones a friend of the Nazis by recontextualizing selective fragments into a seemingly damning confession, leading to the inevitable conclusion: "... without doubt Gareth loved the enemy..."[14]

This peculiar but revealing recontextualization is based on a simple but flawed bifurcation: that if Jones was anti-Soviet, he must have been pro-Nazi. Cherfas asserts, "To be against one meant aligning oneself with the other. The choice defined a generation."[15] By that logic, because Jones exposed mass starvation in the Soviet Union, it follows that his exposé aligned him with Nazi Germany. And because he related in personal correspondence that he found a Jew's manners distasteful or was surprised to discover that a student he had met was a Jew, Jones revealed an unconscious racism. Couched within a false binary, this one-dimensional rendering of his character to answer complex questions delegitimates the importance of his newspaper articles and renders him little more than another antisemitic Hitler stooge. It suggests that anything is possible, a cynical form of historical inquiry in which any narrative is as valid as any other.

Numerous examples illustrate how conveniently the inference of bigotry can be applied. Jones wrote his family a letter recounting a lecture on affairs in the Soviet Union based on his recent visit, at the First Presbyterian Church of Buffalo, New York, in November 1931. "The lights in the Church were very striking and the mass of colours, but it is strange, I can get no affection for the Russians as I have for the Germans."[16] This simple assertion then can be conflated to mean his affection was for Germans who were or became known Nazis. By recontextualizing disparate facts, it's possible to insinuate his affinity for Germany and an affinity for the Nazis were one and the same, as if Jones were incapable of separating them. The question that must be answered then is how and to what extent did any unconscious

8

racism and antisemitic bigotry impact his reporting on the Soviet Union and Nazi Germany? If Jones were a latent Nazi, sympathetic to Hitler's ideology of hatred, those attitudes should permeate his reporting, regardless of what regime he reported on. The easiest way to deny genocide in Ukraine is to associate Jones's reporting with Nazi propaganda.

Jones was far from one-dimensional in his political views. The "Hero of Ukraine" expressed critical views towards White Russians, those who had emigrated before or during the Revolution and now opposed the Soviets. For example, after speaking to a group of Russian students, Jones wrote:

> It went off very well, but I had the feeling when I talked to them – they were White Russians – that they were hopeless at governing, fanatical and unreliable, and I prefer the Communists to the White Russians. I hate the atmosphere of spying and dictatorship that pervades Russian places. It is exciting when one gets first into such an atmosphere, but when one gets used to it becomes very underhand and despicable.[17]

This passage in which he expressed preference for the Communists over White Russians creates an affective discomfort for those who laud Jones's anti-Soviet reporting. Rather than avoiding passages in which Jones criticized one group or another to fit a certain narrative, the point should be that Jones despised an atmosphere of spying and terror wherever he found it, including among White Russians. If the goal of elevating Jones to the status of "Hero of Ukraine" is to create a one-dimensional portrait that readily satisfies all the necessary qualifications to make him the ideal reporter of the *Holodomor*, then that portrait becomes distorted and ultimately unreliable. It is of dubious value and nonsensical to expect that every single opinion Jones expressed must fall within carefully wrought parameters. That forced binary of "for us, against them" creates an expectation of certainty that brings everything into a neatly packaged portrait, convenient but distorted.

Jones's critical estimations were not reserved for only Soviet and German revolutionary dictatorships. He generalized American politicians with a broad, harsh brush. "The political public men

9

of America are of poor calibre. I think the American Congress is a set of the most ignorant humbugs and busybodies in the world."[18] Additionally, Jones considered Poles a "second-rate people" and the French acted like thugs in regions bordering Germany, even though he was as fluent in French as he was in German and Russian. Jones had spent considerable time as a student in France but wrote few newspaper articles about French politics other than how it impacted Germany or the Soviet Union. Jones was certainly opinionated and judgmental, yet while personality contributes to tonal quality in discourse, the many hues applied do not obfuscate the meanings he communicated. Reading Jones is not an exercise in cypher. His writing is direct, analytic, driven by research and sourced anecdotes. The newspaper articles directly expressed what he wanted to communicate, capturing the momentous events of his time.

The purpose of this study is to contextualize Jones's newspaper articles covering Germany between 1930-1934. While most studies of media discourse are "like snapshots examining some news items in detail but covering a short time span,"[19] this project brings focus to several series of newspaper articles that appeared in the *Western Mail*. A time-sensitive analysis means "considering the particular context of a given period, from specific events and developments related to the issue under examination to wider aspects of the social environment."[20] Because Jones was often a participant in his news articles, it's important to consider how he presents conflicting viewpoints, how he dramatizes events, and how he portrays people he meets. Additional primary source material can be found in personal correspondence – the weekly letters to his family – and in his notebook-diaries as they provide corroborating evidence in notes and observations he kept. Only by examining the full body of work related to Germany can we attempt to understand which parts of the competing narratives are found in his work and which are insinuations.

Jones certainly worked diligently to make a name for himself as foreign affairs adviser, journalist, speaker, and gentleman. He wanted nothing more than to have an impact on what was happening in his time, and for that reason he turned down opportunities to teach language and literature. Jones wasn't necessarily interested in having to teach what had already happened; rather, he wanted to represent the world he encountered. That he encountered some of the most impactful historical figures and events of the 1930s is beyond dispute, and his reporting of those events offers considerable insight into what responsible journalism looked like at that time.

'people to see in Berlin'

Despite his exemplary reporting, Jones is completely absent from the numerous studies of the role played by journalists in shaping public opinion about Hitler's rise to power in Nazi Germany. The overarching themes in these books congregate around the Holocaust, failures of the press to sound the alarm, public indifference to foreign affairs, and nationalist fervor stoked by victimization, unemployment, and poverty.[21] That Jones rates absolutely no mention in journalists' memoirs about the time period largely stems from his status as foreign affairs adviser, not full-time correspondent stationed in Berlin. Jones was not a regular at the *Taverne*; however, those journalists stationed in Berlin were important sources of information, and Jones included them among contacts to seek out on any given assignment, as evidenced in this one pocket diary page – "People to see in Berlin" – from February 1933. Included are four key journalists stationed in Berlin including Hubert Renfro Knickerbocker of the *New York Evening Post*, Frederick Voight of the *Manchester Guardian*, Edgar Ansel Mowrer of the *Chicago Daily News*, and Norman Ebbutt of *The Times*. Jones maintained relations with a considerable network of journalists, as well as political, economic, civic, and religious leaders. Knickerbocker and Mowrer broke the story about mass starvation in the Soviet Union on March 29 in Berlin, with Jones as the main source, and the two doubtlessly served as sources for Jones's series about Hitler and the Nazis. This conjunction becomes magnified in light of what is now known. The tendency to focus on one event and country or the other, rather than both parts, creates an incomplete representation.

How Jones has been used to foster recognition of and respect for the *Holodomor* as well as how Jones is portrayed by genocide deniers becomes a critical issue. And because Jones's reporting of

Jones's list of key Berlin-based journalists he wanted to meet, February 1933.

mass starvation in Ukraine was part of a larger series that included Hitler's rise to power, it is important to consider the entire series. Perhaps, then, it is possible to see his work in the context of fundamental human rights, which he believed was a necessary condition for peace and prosperity. Jones, of course, was not the only or the first to write about mass starvation in Ukraine, but he has become the most identifiable. For that, he serves as a viable link to establishing legitimacy of an event which represents a huge part of contemporary Ukrainian identity. Because no one was ever held to account in an international court of justice for crimes committed against Ukrainian people in 1932-33, the victims continue to be denied resolution and historical culture struggles to legitimate the past.

'quite a privileged person'

Before undertaking an analysis of the relevant series of newspaper articles, biographical facts and anecdotes about Jones and Germany provide a particular structuring to the complex relations and experiences that constituted Jones's growth as a person. Jones visited Germany every year from 1923-1934, first as a student at Aberystwyth and then at Trinity College at Cambridge. Interest in politics was formed during this formative time. For example, in one pocket diary from 1923, Jones assiduously took notes in German, recording impressions and interviews. In a letter to his family, he noted that there appeared to be many people in the cafés with plenty of money to spend. "I am told that the Jews are tremendously wealthy and that they have done their best to lower the mark. The lowering of the mark seems to be a game kept up by the German Jews & bankers. Bank buildings are going up everywhere, while the real Germans are poor."[22] That Jones stereotyped wealthy Jews manipulating currency at the expense of real Germans illustrates a prejudicial attitude, despite couching the remark within "I am told." Even though the attribution is a form of distancing from his source, it creates, in this case, a distinction without a difference. Also, aged only 17, he did not have the self-awareness to reject the stereotype. That does not preclude his maturation and adopting different attitudes toward the Jews.

Another important experience was his becoming a conference delegate to the Congress of the International Students (CIE) in Warsaw, Poland, to consider "the political grievances of young men across Europe."[23] Jones understood the growth of Polish nationalism as a response to oppressive measures by the Soviet Union in the East and Nazi Germany in the West. There was a long-simmering hatred of Russian oppression, which barred Polish language being taught in schools. Because of the creation of several nation-states by the Treaty of Versailles, the treatment of minorities within a nation became a key issue for Jones. These impressions had a lasting impact on how he saw Europe as it devolved into nationalistic bigotry.

His mother Annie's experiences in Tsarist Russia in the 1890s while working for Welsh engineer John Hughes, who built part of the Tsar's railroad, impacted him as well. She had been deeply moved by pogroms and other restrictive measures, especially the persecution of Jews. Jones visited a Warsaw ghetto in the Jewish Quarter with a Jewish delegate to the conference, Caplan, and "found it to be dirty and squalid, kept that way purposefully by the Polish Health Department."[24]

In 1926, when Germany was admitted into the League of Nations, Jones visited Geneva as an interested bystander, part of a student delegation from Aberystwyth who attended the plenary session, after which he wrote, "The only way to avoid war was to have the economic conditions of the world controlled by the League of Nations."[25]

Having been accepted into Trinity College, Cambridge University, Jones began hosting regular weekly meetings to which international students were invited to speak about their home countries. His letters chronicle how he worked diligently to achieve Firsts in language courses. His love of travel and meeting people are described in detail, admitting, for example, that his work as a deckhand aboard the SS *Vesta* had turned into something else. "I am having a splendid time on board and am quite a privileged person. I have food with the captain's family...do nothing except stroll about, read, play with little seven-year-old Ella, who is a little Tartar."[26] That journey included excursions into Norway, Germany, and Latvia, where he bought and read a daily newspaper in Russian and advertised himself as an English tutor. The return journey took him from Riga to Stettin aboard the SS *Ostsee* and provided Jones with opportunities to speak German. In a letter home, he recounted meeting a German sailor who had been a prisoner held in Cardiff during World War I.

> He said that the Germans asked Dada [Edgar Jones, his father] if they could do their own cooking instead of having the same food as the other nationalities and that Dada was very decent about it & allowed them to. The sailor said that he was wonderfully treated during the war & did not want to go back to Germany.

In the same letter, Jones described meeting a passenger with whom he got along immensely well.

> He is from the Harz & is the type of German whom I like so much. He has a guitar with him; is dressed in short brown corduroy trousers & open collar. He is also a teetotaler, does not smoke. He & a lot of friends have been visiting the German colonies in Latvia & singing old German folk-songs to them.[27]

Jones, of course, was also a non-smoker and non-drinker, a true Welsh nonconformist, who enjoyed outdoor activities that included alpine climbing, hiking, golfing, skating, and skiing. The passage also illustrates his affinity for folk music and culture.

On another visit to Germany in the summer of 1928, Jones not only toured with the Madrigal Society, but he also studied German history and language at Leipzig University. Unsurprisingly, Jones assumed the role of main translator for the Madrigal Society during the trip. Their tour of Germany included stops in Cologne, where the group visited the *Hohe Domkirche Sankt Petrus* [High Cathedral Church of Saint Peter]. While in Cologne, Jones spent time with Mr. & Mrs. Lowdon, acquaintances that his parents knew and whom he had met in Lyon, France, on previous trips. He spent part of his time with Keith Jopson, who served as a model for people in the consular service. One of his letters was composed on British General-Consulate Cologne stationery: "I am very attracted by the service & by the pay. It is wonderfully interesting work and I cannot imagine a life which would suit me better. I am adaptable and get on well with all classes." Jones was particularly impressed with the salary, as Mr Lowdon had told him the salary was excellent for a bachelor and that the problem was people had married during the war and started a family too quickly. The Lowdons also conveyed to him how "the Germans are generous & hospitable to a fault, but they cannot save. They spend their money straight away. People, who are very poor, give lavish dinners.... I cannot get over the prosperity in Germany. Everybody seems healthy, brown, happy, & contented, compared with the inflation time. But they say that really things are not so good as they appear."[28] After seeing off members of the Madrigal Society, Jones spent time with Haferkorn at Leipzig University to experience university life there.

On the train leaving Cologne, Jones engaged a member of the Sailors Trade Union. "I had a conversation in the train with one of the leaders of the Sailors Trade Union – a very sensible clever, working-man who said he was a colleague of the leader of the German Communist party. He was a big internationalist." The passage illustrates Jones's proclivity for engaging people and learning about them, one of the hallmarks of his reportorial practice. In the same letter, Jones described Frankfurt. "We toured the old part of Frankfurt which was beautifully clean. It is the nicest town in Germany.... Then we had an excellent lunch in a room overlooking the Main in the very same room where [Felix] Mendelssohn celebrated his engagement in 1837. We all stayed with the leading families of the town."[29] That he could relate his experiences to others reveals an emerging sense of history.

Jones spent his time at Leipzig University attending lectures. "I had a very interesting morning, went to 3 lectures, 9 o'clock Borowski on Milton, 10 o'clock to the famous Brandenburg on German History in the 19th c. (excellent, I am going again tomorrow.) At 12, I went to hear another professor lecture on Kant's philosophy. This evening, I am going at 7 to hear Reinhard lecture & at 8:30 to the French Club."[30] That Jones chronicled for his parents the details of his appointments is not surprising given the support they provided him. With Haferkorn serving as guide, Jones acquired first-hand experiences that brought into focus how much he enjoyed Germany. Because of his parents' devotion to education, Jones already understood what a teaching career involved, and on this visit, he learned about Haferkorn's transition to a new position at Danzig Technical College later that fall. However much Jones appreciated the learning environment, he still considered the consular service a better option. On August 1, he called at the consulate, but the consul was away, so he met with the pro-consul. "I talked to the Chief Clerk.... He did not strike me as a very suitable man for the post. He hated the Saxons! The French he loathes like poison! The Czechs are awful people. He likes the Russians and the Germans as a whole, but they are very dull & heavy! I always take with a pinch of salt what people say about other nations & states."[31] Even as Jones matured, he was not immune from forming unflattering opinions about nations and states.

Once Jones found a Russian-speaking student, Braun, with whom he exchanged tutoring sessions, he worked diligently on his Russian language skills as well as German. One of the things that impressed him was seeing an uncut Soviet version of Sergei Eisenstein's film, *Potemkin*. "Like all Soviet films I have seen, it was wonderful in all respects, gripping, photography marvelous. There were no stars; no names of actors were mentioned. The mass-effects were great and you felt as if you were really present." Jones had a keen sense for narrative techniques, and he learned to create a sense of immediacy in his articles by showing people caught in a moment pregnant with meaning. Jones was struck by the gruesome scenes of cruelty perpetrated on innocent people. He noted that the audience cheered when retribution was taken against the officers. "It was cleverly done, the propaganda was very cunningly veiled.

It struck one as very impartial, whereas really is was the most clever kind of propaganda. It has been prohibited in nearly all the countries of Europe. I was most lucky to see it."[32] Jones was equally impressed with a demonstration by Red Front Fighters, noting that women were among those carrying banners as they marched in unison.

Jones also wrote to his family about another experience that Haferkorn introduced of German student life, and it left a less than favorable impression: dueling with rapiers. While Jones thoroughly enjoyed the outdoors in Germany where compulsory sport was practiced, he could not and would not take up arms, even as a sporting gesture. "I thought it all ridiculous and medieval to slash one another with rapiers. It gave me another impression of German student life – a side I don't like at all."[33] Jones was forthright in his criticism, but he did not let one incident distract him from his desire to learn as much as he could.

To commemorate that summer session in Leipzig and Cologne, Jones received a book of poetry from the Haferkorns, dedicated to him. Jones certainly was not above flattery, and always returned favors, invitations, and gifts. The assertion that "the risk he [Jones] ran was that they saw him as 'one of us'"[34] places the blame for how others perceived him unfairly on Jones, as if he were incapable of defining boundaries, though those demarcations are clearly articulated in personal correspondence and his newspaper articles.

Finally, in oral exams, he related speaking perfect French and German. "In the German oral I spoke all the time. The German fellow who examined me seemed so afraid of me that it gave me confidence. I spoke about the German youth movement and other relevant topics for almost 20 minutes without stopping."[35]

'I shall not bind myself'

In addition to being a first-rate linguist, Jones was a multi-faceted individual capable of confronting oppression but also capable of pranks. That he could assume a Zelig-like cast of personas is evidenced in this humorous incident he described for his family.

Ludovick [Stewart] took me in his car to Lingay fens. On the way, he called to take a girl he knew with us. Before going in the house, he said: 'let me introduce you as a Frenchman. What shall I call you?' 'Oh! Call me Count Louzac' I said. I was introduced as a Frenchman and was a great success.... She told Ludovick and Peter Lewis when I was skating far off. 'Your friend Count Louzac is an absolute dear. Where did you pick him up?'[36]

Little wonder that the testimonial references he received from his professors were glowing. One was from Professor Hugh Fraser Stewart, Ludovick's father. "With nimbleness of mind and rapidity, he reached a high first-class standard in every language he studied.... He has a clever head and a retentive memory."[37] Dr Stewart's praise stayed with him, and Jones used a form of this phrase to counter Duranty's derision. His professor of German, Dr. Breul, complimented his fluency in German and his understanding of "modern German life and thought, politics, social and educational questions and conditions and has been for several years in intimate touch with the 'Youth Movement' in Germany and other continental movements."[38] Breul concluded that Jones would do valuable work as a foreign correspondent to a leading newspaper, a member of the Consular Service, or as a staff member of the League of Nations.

Unable to land a position in the Consular Service, Jones accepted a one-month trial at *The Times* in 1929, but not having the requisite experience, he was encouraged to get more journalism experience at a provincial newspaper. His entry into journalism was further delayed when he was introduced to the former Prime Minister David Lloyd George by Dr. Thomas Jones, deputy Cabinet secretary and founder of a monthly journal, *The Welsh Outlook*.

Jones was invited to provide Lloyd George, the former Prime Minister, with information about conditions in Germany, and he so impressed Lloyd George that he was offered a position. Despite Lloyd George's importance as a Welsh stateman, his parents cautioned Jones from a career in politics. Jones responded as he often did by assuaging them. "Please do not worry about it. It is not going into politics, and I shall not bind myself to any fixed political rules. Therefore, I shall be able to be independent and non-political."[39] This final statement asserts his independent spirit; he was non-political only in the sense

18

of not intending to become a political figure. Coverage of political matters, however, resided at the core of his endeavors.

Jones began working on January 1, 1930, as a foreign affairs adviser to Lloyd George. His appointment book for that year provides a detailed list of engagements, meetings, and social outings. In addition to establishing residence at 119 Adelaide Road, Hampstead NW3, a telephone number, and bank savings account with the United Kingdom Temperance & General Provident Institute, Jones regularly attended the Royal Institute of International Affairs (RIIA) lectures, dined out, and enjoyed concerts and dances. He calculated that by age 49 his life insurance policy would be valued at £800 or £40 a year.

Part of his work regime for Lloyd George included reading seven French, one Swiss, two Italian, three German, and four Russian newspapers, as well as the *Chicago Tribune*. Jones quickly became an integral part of Lloyd George's entourage, preparing speeches and briefs, often at a moment's notice, and usually with noteworthy political and economic figures. Despite his busy schedule, Jones managed several weekend trips back to Cambridge, joining groups like the Welsh University Dinner Group and the Russia-Welsh Society among others. Jones stayed in touch with Ludovick Stewart and his sister Margaret, in whom Jones took an interest and with whom he corresponded at particularly key junctures over the next five years.

By August 1930, Jones traveled to the Soviet Union for three weeks, seeing the offices of *Pravda* and *Izvestia*, interviewing people in the Foreign Press Department and the Ministry of Agriculture, who arranged for him to visit collective and state farms in Ukraine. Jones traveled unaccompanied to Rostov and the village where his mother Annie had lived with the Hughes family. The desperate poverty, the lack of food and basic materials, Jones reported to his family in a letter written in Berlin. "Russia is in a very bad state; rotten, no food; oppression, injustice, misery among the workers and 90% discontented. The winter is going to be one of great suffering there and there is starvation. The government is the most brutal in the world. The peasants hate the Communists."[40]

In a few sentences Jones delineated the major themes that dominated his articles covering events in the Soviet Union. The central question for scholars elides from this final trope: Can Jones's

The young Welsh reporter, 1930.

reporting of peasant hatred for the Communists be read as hatred of the Jews? Nazi propaganda demonized the Jew-Bolshevik to engender nationalist hatred in several countries that contributed to pogroms and ultimately to the Final Solution. As Louis P. Lochner, the Associated Press correspondent who spent two decades in Germany, explained, Hitler needed more than an ideology; he needed an opponent against whom he could direct blame and hatred, and the Jew-Bolshevik became this arch enemy. Lochner noted in his memoir, *What About Germany?*, that at the 1935 Nazi Party convention, Joseph Goebbels denounced communism "supported by Jewry" to be "the sworn enemy of all nations, all religions, and all cultures."[41]

Jones's reporting on Nazi Germany takes on increased significance in light of the persecution of Jews in Germany. Analysis of his articles on the Soviets reveals no bias marking Communist Party members as Jews, nor dominant Jewish over-representation within any branch of Soviet bureaucracy, especially the OGPU, the Soviet secret police that exiled any counter-revolutionary suspected of espionage or undermining the Five-Year Plan.[42] Despite examples of stereotyping of Jews in personal correspondence during his school days, Jones's published articles do not suggest anything remotely related to an international Jewish Consortium[43] intent on taking over the world through communism. Despite pointed criticisms about the Soviet Five-Year Plan, Jones even considered studying in the Soviet Union at one point in 1932. His articles about the Soviet Union were certainly not based on stereotypes of the Jew-Bolshevik.

Jones's entry into journalism came as a result of his description of this journey to the Soviet Union at a meeting that included Lloyd

George, Wallace Stewart, Seebohm Rowntree, and Philip Kerr (Lord Lothian) who put him in touch with Geoffrey Dawson, editor of *The Times*. Jones's work was published in a variety of newspaper and journals, but it was not until April 1, 1933, that Jones accepted a full-time position with the *Western Mail* in Cardiff, Wales, and he ended it 17 months later when on October 1, 1934, he declared himself a free man. Jones chose to go it alone as a freelance journalist on his round the world tour, and that, in effect, defines him forever – on assignment.

Notes

1 Theresa Cherfas, "'Germany, my Beloved Land' Gareth Jones and the Nazis," *Planet: The Welsh Internationalist*, 210 (Summer 2013), 76.

2 Gareth Jones, Letter date June 18, 1933. Gareth Vaughan Jones Papers, National Library of Wales, File B6/5.

3 Gareth Jones, "Primitive Worship of Hitler, *Western Mail*, March 2, 1933, 13.

4 Wilhelm J. Wiss, Letter dated September 2, 1935. Quoted in Cherfas, 67.

5 Ray Gamache, "Breaking Eggs for a Holodomor: Walter Duranty, *New York Times*, and the Denigration of Gareth Jones," *Journalism History*, 39:4 (Winter 2014), 208-218.

6. See Ray Gamache, "Contextualizing FDR's Campaign to Recognize the Soviet Union, 1932-1933: Propaganda, Genocide Denial, and Ukrainian Resistance," *Harvard Ukrainian Studies Journal*, 37(2), n.p.

7 Gareth Jones, Letter to the Editor – Mr. Jones Replies, *New York Times*, May 13, 1933, 12.

8 Jones, Letter to the Editor, 13.

9 Eugene Lyons, *Assignment in Utopia* (New York: Harcourt, Brace and Company, 1937), 575-576.

10 Lawrence Grossberg, "Reality Is Bad Enough, Draft Chapter One." Accessed from https://www.researchgate.net/publication/321805684_REALITY_IS_BAD_ENOUGH_DRAFT_CHAPTER_ONE?channel=doi&linkId=5a32a57b0f7e9b2a287c1c41&showFulltext=true.

11 Grossberg, "Reality Is Bad Enough," 24-25.

12 Anabela Carvalho, "Media(ted) Discourse and Society," *Journalism Studies*, 2008, 9(2), 161-177.

13 Carvalho, "Media(ted)," 172.

14 Cherfas, "My Beloved Land," 67.

15 Cherfas, "My Beloved Land," 77.

16 Gareth Jones, Letter dated November 1931. Gareth Vaughan Jones Papers, National Library of Wales, File B6/3.

17 Gareth Jones, Letter dated November 1931.

18 Gareth Jones, Letter dated April 17, 1932. Gareth Vaughan Jones Papers, National Library of Wales, File B6/3.

19 Carvalho, "Media(ted)," 164.

20 Carvalho, "Media(ted), 164.

21 The Taverne figures prominently in Will Wainewright, *Reporting on Hitler: Rothay Reynolds and the British Press in Nazi Germany* (London: Biteback Publishing, 2017), 109-127; and Daniel Schneidermann, *Berlin, 1933: La Presse Internationale Face à Hitler* (Paris: Editions du Seuil, 2018).

22 Gareth Jones, Letter dated July 15, 1923. Gareth Vaughan Jones Papers, National Library of Wales, File B6/1.

23 Dr. Margaret Siriol Colley, *More Than a Grain of Truth: The Biography of Gareth Richard Vaughan Jones* (Newark, Nottinghamshire, 2005), 21.

24 Colley, *More Than a Grain*, 10.

25 Quoted in Colley, *More Than a Grain*, 14.

26 Gareth Jones, Letter dated July 8, 1927. Gareth Vaughan Jones Papers, National Library of Wales, File B6/1.

27 Gareth Jones, Letter dated August 16, 1927. Gareth Vaughan Jones Papers, National Library of Wales, File B6/1.

28 Gareth Jones, Letter dated July 12, 1928. Gareth Vaughan Jones Papers, National Library of Wales, File B6/1.

29 Gareth Jones, Letter dated February 1929. Gareth Vaughan Jones Papers, National Library of Wales, File B6/2.

30 Gareth Jones, Letter dated July 18, 1928. Gareth Vaughan Jones Papers, National Library of Wales, File B6/1.

31 Gareth Jones, Letter dated August 1, 1928. Gareth Vaughan Jones Papers, National Library of Wales, File B6/1.

32 Gareth Jones, Letter dated July 18, 1928.

33 Gareth Jones, Letter dated July 22, 1928. Gareth Vaughan Jones Papers, National Library of Wales, File B6/1.

34 Cherfas, "My Beloved Land," 73.

35 Gareth Jones, Letter dated June 1928. Gareth Vaughan Jones Papers, National Library of Wales, File B6/1.

36 Gareth Jones, Letter dated February 1929. Gareth Vaughan Jones Papers, National Library of Wales, File B6/2.

37 Quoted in Colley, *More Than a Grain*, 45.

38 Quoted in Colley, *More Than a Grain*, 46.

39 Gareth Jones, Letter dated October 28, 1929. Gareth Vaughan Jones Papers, National Library of Wales, File B6/2.

40 Gareth Jones, Letter dated August 26, 1930. Gareth Vaughan Jones Papers, National Library of Wales, Folder 16.

41 Louis P. Lochner, *What About Germany?* (New York: Dodd, Mead & Company, 1942), 10, 19.

42 Ray Gamache, *Gareth Jones: Eyewitness to the Holodomor* (Cardiff, Wales: Welsh Academic Press, 2013).

43 See Kris Dietrich, *Taboo Genocide: 1933 & the Extermination of Ukraine – Volume II.* (Xlibris, 2015). Volume II is subtitled, The Never Before Told Story of the Anglo-American Consortium & the 1933 Terror-Famine in Soviet Ukraine. This typifies the antisemitic trope of a Jew-Bolshevik conspiracy to take control of the world. This encyclopedia or compendium brings together such information overload as to drown out the very narrative it seeks to represent. As Mark Andrejevic notes in his book *Infoglut,* "It is not just that there is information available, but that this surfeit has highlighted the incompleteness of any individual account. An era of information coincides, in other words, with the reflexive recognition of the constructed and partial nature of representation." Gareth Jones appears on the opening page of Dietrich's xenophobic tome.

2

A Real Menace

'hooliganistic methods'

Shortly after Jones returned from his first journey to the Soviet Union in August 1930, he turned his attention to one of the worldwide concerns for the coming year, unemployment. Jones skillfully offered a composite picture of what happened to workers. "He has no name for he exists in nearly all countries. He is the victim of 1930, the Unemployed."[1] While this composite character reflected a myriad of feelings, anger had taken root in the pit of his empty stomach, cursing "against the world order as he hears of over-production of wheat and butter, of cloth and manufactured goods, and cannot get any himself."[2]

In one paragraph, Jones outlined one important trope of his reporting as he focused on poverty due to the failure of political establishments. Hunger and starvation at a time of the world's greatest surplus of wheat became central to his journalistic endeavors to advocate for basic human rights. Having access to important political figures, labor leaders, and economists, Jones spent most of his time researching the issues of the day, and his language and communication skills, honed in Aberystwyth, Cambridge, and Strasbourg meant he could engage with Europeans on their own terms – in French, German and Russian – thus bypassing any linguistic or cultural impediment to move freely through any environment.

Describing the plight of the German unemployed worker, Jones noted that four million men and women were barred from factories and mines, giving rise to "fear, hatred, depression and despair in the dealings of nations.... There has been talk of WAR." The German complaint had by the end of 1930 become clear, as Jones quoted a man who said "what all Germans are thinking. 'The French promised to disarm and they are as powerful as ever. We cannot stick any longer being treated as we are and kept prisoners by the French generals and politicians. Every German would willingly die to win the Polish Corridor back."[3]

This distinctly German sentiment Jones conveyed as an argument that had already been debated and clearly formulated to mean that Germany must build up her army and navy to defend what was rightfully hers. Jones came across that very same sentiment again in February 1933 when he noted seeing a movie poster. "I would die ten times, a hundred times for Germany." "Brother, why rejoice? They were doing their duty and they have sent to their death many people who were also only doing their duty."[4] This distinctly anti-war message Jones would have agreed with as he became more involved with pacifist groups like *Brüder in Not* [Brothers in Need].

In several articles Jones wrote over the next four years about Germany, the problem of Danzig and the Polish Corridor remained a source of intense speculation. Jones noted that it was a rallying cry for young German people. "Hitlerites with their hooliganistic methods and their aims of a powerful armed Germany are growing from day to day and are going to be before long a real menace."[5] The Nazis were offering Germans hope about overcoming the unfair conditions meted out after World War I in the form of reparations for atrocities committed only in Entente propaganda.

This first published reference to Hitler and the Nazis leaves little doubt as to what Jones initially thought about them, especially their brutal but efficient methods. Despite having a deep abiding love of Germany, Jones distinguished Nazi ideology from native characteristics, deluding people into wanting revenge. "Everywhere Liberalism and Democracy are rolled in mud, and everywhere the herd is shouting for the strong guidance of one firm leader."[6]

Jones understood that for many Germans the need for someone to right the wrongs never seemed more obvious. Nazi propaganda hammered at the failures of the Treaty of Versailles and the League of Nations, and when the government of Chancellor Hermann Müller collapsed in March, President Paul von Hindenburg appointed Heinrich Brüning to form a minority government that failed to enact the measures needed to stabilize the German economy. By July, Brüning attempted to force through unpopular measures to tighten credit and freeze wages with an emergency decree, but a coalition defeated the measure, forcing Brüning to ask Hindenburg to dissolve the Reichstag and call for new elections. That Hitler was primed to capitalize on Germany's disillusioned masses became evident to Jones. The federal elections of September 14, 1930, confirmed that disillusionment when the Nazis increased Reichstag representation from a mere dozen to 107, to become the second largest bloc behind the Social Democratic Party's 143 members but more than the Communist Party of Germany's (KPD) 77 members.

Having worked so intently with David Lloyd George, a signatoree to the Treaty of Versailles, Jones understood what was at stake, a fragile peace beginning to fall apart because of a worsening worldwide depression. "Next year will be a critical one for the League. If it does nothing to persuade the nations to disarm and if it leaves Germany weak amidst powerful States, then hatred of the League will become violent in Germany and might even force Germany to leave."

Germany's entry into the League in 1926 had accomplished little to stabilize its faltering economy, saddled with reparations and war debts that exacerbated inflation and created disillusion. Despite having created "a picture of black-threatening clouds," a description he used again in a later series on Germany, Jones concluded the article by offering one hopeful ray of light in what the League was doing to promote cooperation between nations. "They are learning the lesson that loving one's neighbour is practical politics. Then the fact that the hard-headed business man is on the side of peace and is developing international cartels is a bright sign."[7] As a professed pacifist, Jones tolerated "the hard-headed business man" as long as prosperity engendered peace, but his enthusiasm waned whenever he encountered the dire conditions workers and craftsmen had to endure.

'self in window'

Jones also found a hopeful gleam in "our friendship with America. It is not long ago that people were predicting war with America."[8] Pointing to the London Naval Conference, Jones advocated that relations with the United States offered the best prospects for peace. In April 1931, Jones sailed to the States aboard the *Île de France* with Ivy Ledbetter Lee, the public relations specialist who had hired him to ghost write a book about the Soviet Union. Lee had advocated for recognition of the Soviet Union since 1926 when he responded to the Chamber of Commerce of New York's campaign never to recognize the Soviet Union as long as the Communist Party was in control. Lee believed that only open and frank exchanges could stimulate understanding. That Jones had recently visited the Soviet Union made him a valuable resource for Lee. The reports Jones researched and wrote for Lee constituted important source material that he often re-incorporated into his journalistic work.

Before departing for the United States, Jones took a trip to Germany and Poland in early January 1931 to assess what was happening in the Polish Corridor. Jones kept a notebook of his impressions, written in German with only a few pages in English, recording his interviews with a number of German and Polish leaders. He even sent his family newspaper clippings following his visit to *Wilhelmstrasse*. Jones wrote on it, "President's reception. X = self in window. Can you recognise me?" In the second one, he marked a spot xx and wrote, "My taxi stopped here and the whole crowd stares as if I were an Ambassador."[9]

That Jones had gained entrée into the highest levels of government is evident in his having seen the leading ministers of the German Foreign Office and all the diplomats from a window on the ground floor of the President's Palace, a guest at President Hindenburg's reception. Soon after this episode, while in Washington, D.C., Jones cleverly barged in on a White House event to which he was not party and ended up having his picture taken with President Herbert Hoover. Jones possessed the communication skills that allowed him considerable access to the political elite. With his calling card, backed by Lloyd George or Ivy Lee, Jones went wherever he wanted.

Die Anfahrt in der Wilhelmstraße.

xx My taxi stopped here
and the whole crowd stared as
if I were an Ambassador.

A German newspaper clipping marked by Jones, with xx, to show where his taxi stopped, "and the whole crown stared as if I were an Ambassador".

Die Ehrenwache präsentiert.

President's
Palace.

President's
reception.
x = self in window,
can you recognise me?

Another German newspaper clipping marked by Jones, with x, to show "self in window" at the President's reception, 1931.

In that same letter to his family from Germany, Jones related that he had interviewed the German Foreign Minister, Dr. Julius Curtius, at the villa of the Foreign Ministry for almost an hour. "I had heaps of interviews with the Ministerial directors at the Foreign Office, with Dr. [Friedrich] Gaus, who was responsible for Locarno. On Friday also I had a long interview with Count Harry Kessler, a very well-known ex-diplomat, writer and gentleman. All are exceedingly pessimistic about the state of Europe."[10] Jones's letters to his family are striking in the level of detail he provided about his work. They provide candid, unvarnished details to corroborate his travels, his seemingly vast network of contacts, and a catalogue of meals, accommodations, and events.

'a nut in a nutcracker' I

From Germany, Jones next traveled to Poland, where he wrote from the Hotel Monopol, Katowice, where he witnessed a demonstration of unemployed people. "Chleba! Chleba!" ["Bread! Bread!"] he recorded in his notebook, "police drive them away." The notebook was used to record his interview with the governor of Katowice, Mr. [Michal] Grazynski, and served as the basis for his analytical article published in *The Contemporary Review*, titled "Poland's Foreign Relations."[11]

Jones contextualized those relations by describing Poland's geographical position, history of oppression, and economic structure. Two additional factors, international finance and the Catholic Church, also impacted Poland's foreign relations. Those relations, especially with Germany, had increased "the anxiety for security which Poland's geographical position and her past inspire her citizens. The rush of extreme nationalism in Germany, the Nazi cry for a strong conscript army and the revolt of German youth against Versailles, have made the Poles guard their security more tenaciously than ever."[12]

As Jones explained, Poland felt no security on either her western or eastern borders, despite signing the Litvinov Protocol (1929) for the Renunciation of War. In effect, Poland was a perfect propaganda foil for the Communist Party to unite peoples within the Soviet Union "in the face of the so-called menace of intervention from Poland. It is the belief of Moscow that war between the capitalist states and Communist Russia is inevitable and that Poland is to be the catspaw of France, America, and Britain."[13]

Even less auspicious was finding acceptable resolutions to disputes with Germany over the Polish Corridor. Grazynski was the likely source for these ideas, as well as the forecast of trouble: "If Germany regains her pre-war territory, then she will be able to join with Russia through Lithuania and we will be like a nut in a nutcracker, surrounded on almost all sides by hostile neighbours. We are willing to do anything to have good relations with Germany except commit suicide."[14] Jones heard the very same 'nut in a nutcracker' comparison from a Yugoslavian customs official in 1934 when he covered the Nazi assassination of Dollfuss.

Jones predicted that stabilization of the status quo contained seeds for future strife, based on a bifurcation of Europe in opposing camps – one seeking revision to the Treaty of Versailles and the other desiring crystallization of present frontiers. Most alarming to Jones was the treatment of minorities in Poland, thanks in large part to the "utmost rigour and brutality ... by a hooded dictatorship and Pilsudski has been the real force behind the scenes." Jones decried the sham election, which concentrated power in Josez Pilsudski's government and left the areas of Poland inhabited by Germans and Ukrainians to suffer repression. "German-speaking people are placed under a disadvantage in the use of their language. By the Agrarian Reform, the Polish authorities have been able to Polonise the former German districts and to divide the estates of German landowners among Polish peasants." Jones accused the Pilsudski Bloc of violent acts against the Germans, led by "none other than the Woievode himself, Dr. Grazynski. The efforts to secure a victory for the Government Block at all costs and the methods of the 'Insurgents' led to a considerable fall in the German vote."[15]

In terms of Ukraine, Jones characterized its struggle with Poland as one driven by "the jealousy of one social class for another.... The oppression of the Ukrainians takes on a more serious aspect when we remember that in that remote corner is the frontier between Soviet Russia and the rest of Europe. The five to seven million Ukrainians in Poland have twenty-five to thirty million fellow-countrymen across the border. On the Soviet side of the frontier, although any anti-Communist independence movement is instantly crushed, every effort is made to encourage the Ukrainian language, literature, schools and art."

Jones pointed out that paramilitary groups like the Ukrainian Military Organization were working by illegal means for independence. "It is accused of receiving funds from Berlin. Last autumn it started on a campaign which led to the burning of Polish cottages and barns." Jones reiterated that such actions readily became propaganda for the Soviets to create "in lurid terms the fate of oppressed peasants in Poland."[16] The idea of a counter-revolutionary separatist movement of Ukrainians became an important Soviet propaganda weapon to counter reports of mass starvation.

Jones concluded his analysis of Poland's foreign relations by turning from the gloomy outlook involving Germany and the Soviet Union to brighter prospects among agricultural states along its southern border in an attempt to answer questions related to agricultural credits and the disposal of surplus grain stocks. Jones noted, "It is significant that agricultural countries stretching from the Baltic to the Black Sea should have come together and this has been to no small degree facilitated by the wise and far-sighted efforts of the Polish Government."[17] That Jones was already pointing to this surplus of wheat as one of the major stumbling blocks to solving distressed grain prices testifies to his acumen on the subject.

'a triumph of unforeseen magnitude'

After accompanying Jack Heinz, grandson of the American entrepreneur H. J. Heinz and a client of Ivy Lee, on a tour of the Soviet Union in early autumn 1931, Jones transitioned from writing about starving peasants, disgruntled workers, and the brutality of dekulakization to the deepening economic crisis in Germany that was ruining private businesses, the bulwark of a capitalist economy. "A great class has been annihilated, the German middle class. Their savings swept away by the inflation, educated Germans have been reduced to proletarian conditions."

Jones conjoined the decimation of the German middle class with the rise in popularity of Hitler's National Socialist Party that "had gained a triumph of unforeseen magnitude." Desperation and despair fueled this Nazi triumph, but Jones questioned whether or not Hitler could last. A year later conditions had deteriorated to the point that "Germany's capacity to pay has come to an end and rapid action must be taken."[18]

Jones then wrote two articles about the worldwide banking crisis, one for William Randolph Hearst's *New York American* and the other for the *Western Mail*. The Hearst article, "Fascist Dictatorship for Germany Now Possibility, Development," was published on November 29, 1931, and analyzed the causes of Germany's economic upheaval – reparation payments and over-borrowing. While Germany was to blame for the latter, Jones argued, "It is false to accuse Germany of financial bad faith, because the German Reichsbank and the German treasury uttered solemn warnings that too much money was going to German states and municipalities."[18] Those unheeded warnings precipitated "an almost intolerable burden of taxation.... The suffering in Germany is no bluff."[19]

The points Jones discussed centered around debts both private and public, and he offered two suggestions: it was better to be "Against reparations and for private debts" and to "Scrap Tariffs." In the end, Jones recognized that Hitler had become an inevitability which might lead to civil war, perhaps even Bolshevism in Germany. "A Nazi dictatorship in the Spring seems inevitable.... Those are problems we may soon have to face."[20]

In "The World in 1931: A Retrospective of the Banking Crisis," Jones created a dramatic scene set on Berlin's most famous and elegant street, on which could be heard "a pale-faced, white collared clerk shrieking hysterically, 'We've been betrayed! We've been betrayed by the capitalists and betrayed by the Versailles Powers. The capitalists and the French are out for our blood! We've not got enough bread and next year it will be worse. It's New Year's Day tomorrow and I tell you it will dawn on the worst year since the war.'"[21]

This soliloquy typifies Jones's technique, evident in any number of stories, in which he allows a character, here the German middle-class clerk, to articulate grievances that Jones knew resonated with many other unemployed. Jones distilled the key issues in this one brief dramatic shriek, explaining how 1931 became "a hunger year, a hunger year."

Jones structured the tragedy in two parts, decimation of world trade and the Treaty of Versailles. "Deeper and deeper sank the prices of wheat and cotton, steel and copper, sugar and coffee. Heavier and heavier became the burden of international debts." The use of repetition to reinforce intensity was common for Jones, and editors allowed him considerable latitude to explain economic and political conflicts. In the second part, Jones compared the banking crisis to the assassination of Archduke Ferdinand. "Just as a pistol shot in Serbia in 1914 was to set Europe afire, so a little spark in a small country, Austria, was to set aflame to the financial framework of the world." In this case, France was portrayed as pointing a pistol at the Austrian government, extorting with conditions that "would have made Austria almost into a vassal State of France."[22]

Even though the Bank of England stepped in and U. S. President Herbert Hoover emerged to save Austria momentarily, the crisis deepened when "the gold rush continued to drain Germany, causing the downfall of one of her greatest banks." One by one, nations contracted what Jones called "economic diseases" and ultimately their economies came crashing down, forcing them off the gold standard. Jones concluded the article by noting that Japan had taken advantage of the European crisis by sending troops into Manchuria while "the forces of Hitler, the Fascist, mounted in Germany." Jones posed questions about what those "rumblings of disaster" might portend: "Will they save Germany, and thus the world? Or will Germany collapse and bring down the whole economic structure, which gives us bread and shelter? What is now a grim mystery, 1932 will reveal."[23]

Jones clearly juxtaposed the safety and security of the world with Germany's interests in shedding itself of war reparations and debts. If the capitalists failed to find a way to overcome stifling tariffs and embargoes, to generate free trade and stabilize commodity prices, and to provide easy lending policies, then governments faced the uncertainties of unfettered, fascist dictatorships.

'so profound the rebellion'

Those ideas were echoed in a speech that Jones prepared for Ivy Lee in February 1932, "Publication of War Debts & Gold Crisis," delivered at DePauw University, Greencastle, Indiana. Lee, for whom Jones had worked since April 1931, had soured on Europe and Russia in January 1932 at a time when recognition of the Soviet Union was still in the balance and Hitler was gaining even more traction in Germany. Several passages in the speech include information Jones gleaned in his research.

"The Committee of Experts which in 1924 promulgated the Dawes Plan pointed out that payments of reparations by Germany could be made only through bringing about a restoration of German prosperity, particularly in her foreign trade."[24] With this kind of advocacy Jones brought focus to the ongoing dilemma between debts and reparations.

Another idea Jones included related to the War Guilt Lie.

> Regarding, as they have a right to do, this war-guilt accusation as the corner-stone of reparations, the German Consciousness rebels against the plan of reparations to just the extent that this war guilt accusation is regarded as unjust.... The youth of Germany today feels that it is in bondage, that the scheme of reparations deprives the German of opportunity to enjoy life or to attain progress. That feeling is the basis of Hitlerism. So bitter is the feeling, so profound the rebellion against this sense of bondage, that it is hardly possible that the plan of reparations, at least as now imposed, will be long endured by the population of Germany.[25]

Some of this information derived from the time of his oral exams for which he had studied the German Youth Movement.

The passage also evoked a sentiment espoused by Lloyd George in the first volume of *War Memoirs*, which Jones helped prepare. Lloyd George believed that it was a mistake "to attribute exceptional wickedness to the governments" who stumbled into the war. By arguing that Germany should not alone shoulder the blame for the war, Lloyd George countered clauses in the Reparations Chapter of the Treaty. In his speech, Lee made a similar argument. "The scheme of reparations is set forth in the Treaty of Versailles to which Germany was compelled, at the mouths of Allied guns, to sign her name."[26] Jones clearly understood that threatening with violence only increased German resolve to rebuild a strong military force.

In February, Jones sent Lloyd George two papers for inclusion in his book, *The Truth about Reparations and War Debts,* with contributions from "a friend in the United States". While not completely misleading, this representation hardly reaches candidness as Jones's views were decidedly in line with Lloyd George's and were certainly not those prevalent in America. Jones traveled to New England where he lectured, not surprisingly, on "Revision of the Treaty of Versailles" and "The Polish Corridor Problem." Jones advocated for a revised version of the Treaty because its current provisions strangled Germany's economy.

'with a vengeance'

Jones recognized that Lee could not afford to keep him on his staff and, by February, Jones wrote to his family that he was to be let go. "I am making all kinds of plans – going to Chicago – going on a lecture tour – joining Lloyd George again – writing a book on Hitler – writing articles so I will be fine." This attempt to reassure his family was not completely convincing, and in early March, after he'd already made up his mind to return to Lloyd George's staff, he offered this mild rebuke. "I really cannot understand your point of view – to be research adviser on foreign affairs to the former Prime Minister of Great Britain! And you'd refuse it!!!!!!!!!! It's the very thing that has brought me any reputation I may have, and I jolly well think it is an honour and a compliment to be asked back again."[27]

After he had returned to Wales and was working for Lloyd George, Jones emphasized in another letter the importance of what he was doing. "After tea I had a talk with L.G. about my going to Germany. He wants me to go and see [General Erich] Ludendorff! and many people who were connected with the war, for his *Memoirs.* Isn't that entering into the pages of history with a vengeance!... Tomorrow I shall go to Craig's Court to meet the Welsh luncheon group. Perhaps I'll see Sir Percy."[28] The letters reveal that for all their cordiality, Jones was not afraid of asserting himself in going against family wishes. That said, Jones remained committed to family love and loyalty above all else. Jones's desire to make a difference in his work – whether as a foreign affairs adviser or journalist – is clearly expressed in his assertion about entering the pages of history.

Jones did not journey to Germany as he had intimated in his letter. Instead he traveled to Rome, Geneva, and Lausanne, where representatives from several nations discussed the issue of disarmament and an end to war reparations. Neither he nor Lloyd George expected much to come out of the Lausanne Conference. From *Le Grand Hotel* in Rome, Jones wrote: "Mussolini is building roads, bridges, canals, and viaducts in many parts of Italy. He aims at the re-building of his native country, and it is remarkable that his programme follows the lines laid down by the Liberal Party in Great Britain and almost identical with Lloyd George's Liberal plans! What irony that the enemy of Democracy should be carrying out the policy advocated by British Liberals."[29] Jones could not have been surprised when Lloyd George praised both Stalin and Mussolini, but only a year later Jones criticized that admiration of Stalin.

This passage illustrates the quandary for Liberals, who were advocating public works projects similar to those enacted by the fascists in Italy and by Hitler's Nazis in Germany, and by FDR's New Deal in the United States. While the end goal of stimulating national economic activity was central to all, the means of effecting change were strikingly different, especially as Stalin, Mussolini, and Hitler consolidated power.

'no better way'

When on assignment in London, Jones often made home base the Reform Club where Jones had easy access to political and journalist contacts. In mid-July, he was contacted by Paul Scheffer, who telephoned "to ask if I had heard of the disgraceful Gentleman's Agreement at Lausanne which spoils everything.... It ended by receiving an invitation from Hitler's private secretary to join Hitler's private aeroplane party on his election tour at the end of July. Ernst Hanfstaengl, Hitler Foreign Press Chief, has written me a letter saying that there could be no better way than if I join the chief's aeroplane party during the coming election tour."[30] Most likely, this was in response to Jones's inquiry, first mentioned in a May 30 letter to his family that he had written to Hitler's secretary. Jones missed this opportunity which other journalists like Sefton Delmer seized upon to ramp up coverage. Nonetheless, Jones appeared genuinely pleased about the invitation from Hanfstaengl, born to an American mother and educated at Harvard University, who employed American campaign methods that relied on spectacle to invigorate Nazi rallies.[31] Hanfstaengl's July election tour, characterized by uncertainty and occasional confrontations with the KPD, would have revealed how highly charged conditions had become. By February 1933, Jones witnessed first-hand a Nazi rally at Frankfurt, thanks to Hanfstaengl.

Jones briefly traveled to Cambridge to visit the Stewarts in May and then to Wales during the late summer 1932, but he returned to London in August where he met with Haferkorn, who had arrived for a prolonged stay in Great Britain. In October, Haferkorn lectured at the Royal Institute of International Affairs, and Jones hosted an event at the Reform Club prior to the presentation. Jones described Haferkorn's presentation, titled "Danzig and the Polish Corridor," as "clear and short, and the debate which followed was fine.... The RIIA was very pleased, as everything went off excellently, and I was very pleased, as I was responsible."[32]

Haferkorn subsequently introduced Jones to Wolf von Dewall, editor of the *Frankfurter Zeitung*, a liberal German newspaper. Jones lunched with Dewall, his wife, and brother, whom he found charming. "Dewall is a great German correspondent and I liked his wife and his brother. We got on wonderfully together and we have planned tramps."[33] For Jones, cultivating his network of contacts was the means he used to gain access to the leading political figures in Italy, Germany, Poland, the Soviet Union, and the United States.

Prior to writing two provocative articles, titled "Will There Be Soup?" for the *Western Mail* about starvation conditions in the Soviet Union, Jones met with Harvard University Professor Bruce Hopper and Professor Jules Menken of the London School of Economics, who

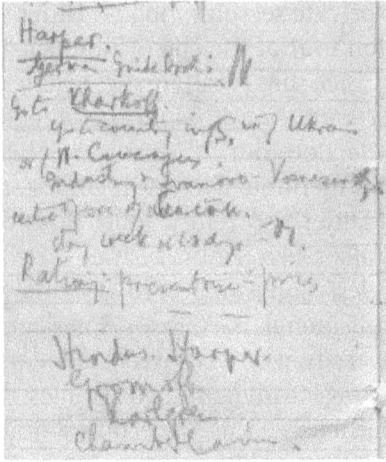

A notebook entry detailing a conversation Jones had with Samuel N. Harper, the noted American scholar, who had recently returned from the Soviet Union.

had recently published articles in *The Economist* that elicited Soviet concerns. Having heard from two experts whom he trusted and having read recent issues of Soviet newspapers, Jones arguably hatched the idea of returning to the Soviet Union to study conditions, even though travel beyond Moscow required permission from the Foreign Press Department. The meeting that prompted Jones to put a plan into place occurred later that fall at the RIIA where Jones met Samuel N. Harper. The first page of a notebook-diary contains instructions that correspond with his trip to the Soviet Union in March.

Harper
>   German guide book
> Go to Kharkoff.
> Go to country in S. in Ukraine or the N. Caucasus.
>>   Stay week or ten days.
>>   Rationing – prevent rise in prices.
> Hindus Harper
> Gromoff
> Karlgren
> Chamberlain.[34]

Additionally, on the facing page are the names and addresses of Russian emigres living in Paris, many of whom Jones interviewed at some point. These contact entries are definitely not in Jones's handwriting, so they were provided to him. They include Alexander Kerensky and Russian Orthodox Church leaders.

Consistently, when Jones underlined a name, the information that followed came directly from that source, so clearly the idea to visit Khar'kiv, Ukraine, and spend a week or more there, came from Samuel Northrup Harper, arguably one of the most experienced researchers on Russia, and a colleague of Sir Bernard Pares. In late October 1932 Harper returned from a visit to the Soviet Union and in early December met with Pares in London in advance of his presentation at the Royal Institute of International Affairs, titled "The Development of Institutions of Government in the USSR." In his diary for December 14, 1932, Jones noted, "RIIA Harper USSR."[35] This brief note provides more documentary evidence that Jones, after attending Harper's lecture and having a brief conversation with him, decided to go to Ukraine on Harper's recommendation, with the specific instruction to spend a week or more in Khar'kiv to study conditions.

Jones's diary and notebook entries can be further corroborated by a U. S. State Department despatch dated October 27, 1932, from the legation in Riga, Latvia, summarizing Harper's visit. Marked "Strictly Confidential" and prepared by Robert Skinner, the notes detail Harper's remarks on the dire state of Soviet agriculture. "The food shortage has become very serious and may become catastrophic in a year from now if no improvement takes place. Worst of all is the situation in Ukraine which last year has been milked dry by the excessive government grain procurements."[36] Of course, Jones had already evidenced, with Heinz, the dire conditions among villagers and farmers whose rations had been severely diminished.

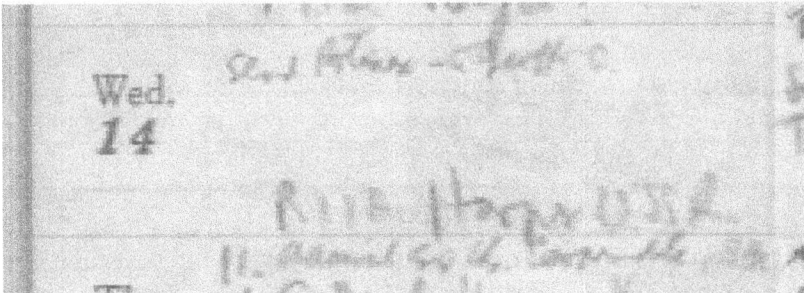

Jones's appointment diary for December 14, 1932, showing Harper's scheduled speech at the RIIA.

```
Enclosure No. 1     to despatch No. 871 of OCT 27 1932
    from the Legation at Riga, Latvia.

STRICTLY CONFIDENTIAL.

    NOTES ON A CONVERSATION WITH PROFESSOR SAMUEL N.
                         HARPER.

Mr. Harper's visit to Russia lasted this time two
```

A US State Department despatch, dated October 27, 1932, summarizing Harper's journey to the Soviet Union.

Jones forwarded his sources' concerns in a letter to Ivy Lee. "The Soviet Government is facing the worst crisis since 1921. The harvest is a failure, and there will be millions facing starvation this winter. There is at the present moment a famine in the Ukraine.... Hopper is suspicious as to the amount of Soviet gold supply, and is afraid the Soviet Union will not meet its obligations."[37] When Lee responded with a pro-Soviet memorandum a week before Jones's articles appeared on October 15-16, Jones responded in no uncertain terms. "I believe that at the present moment, as a result of food shortage, and breakdown of grain plans, there are many people starving in many parts of Russia.... Finally, it would be impossible to increase the productivity of the land through collective farms, on account of the great massacre of horses and cattle."[38]

At this point, Jones's attention focused on conditions in both Germany and the Soviet Union. Jones saw an opportunity to explore the two nations, whose revolutions offered alternatives to a capitalist system, which were now shackled by unemployment and a banking crisis. Jones put a plan into motion that today would be any journalist's dream assignment: ride in Adolph Hitler's airplane to attend a Nazi rally, then travel to Moscow, board a train to Ukraine, tramp through the Ukrainian countryside, and become eyewitness to the most horrific catastrophe in human history up to that time, the mass starvation of four million people.

When and how Jones came to create his series titled "A Welshman Looks at Europe" can be extracted from his correspondence during the period between October 1932 and January 1933. Significantly, by the time the *Western Mail* published the first article, the stated goal was to have Jones cover events in both countries; this was to be one grand series – 12 articles about Nazi Germany and ten articles about the Soviet Union – that garnered considerable recognition for Jones, the foreign affairs adviser from Barry who was still not a full-time journalist.

'people who parade in the very best clothes'

Jones decided to travel to Cologne, Germany, in December 1932. He wrote to his family: "Dewall was in the same class as [Kurt von] Schleicher in school. Schleicher was then a nervous timid little harmless fellow. Now he is Chancellor of Germany. I intend to go to Germany a week next Friday. Berlin is hundreds & hundreds of miles further than Cologne. I have been to Germany every year since 1923, and I do not want to break the 10-year record. It would be good for me as a so-called 'expert'. I shall see as many people as possible; write a couple of articles; a report for Ivy Lee. These will pay my expenses."[39] Jones was intent on getting back into German political affairs, and Schleicher's ascension to the post of chancellor in November 1932 provided the opportunity.

Working from notes kept in another pocket diary, the report Jones prepared for Lee was a comprehensive piece covering Schleicher's programme, the purported decline of the Nazis, German unemployment, the general economic situation,

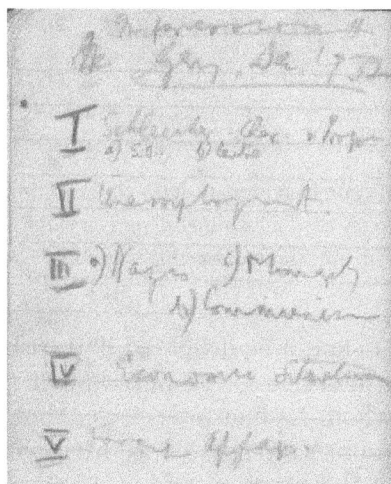

Jones's notebook entry outlining the memo he'd write for Ivy Lee, titled "Impressions of Germany, December 1932".

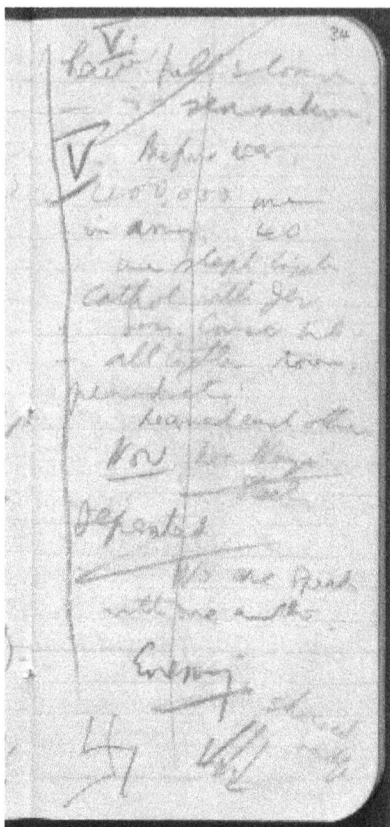

A notebook entry with information Jones used for an memo on Germany's Foreign Affairs, December 1932.

and the outlook on foreign affairs. On the very last page, he created an outline for Lee, which he titled "Impressions of Germany, December 1932". The report is significant in outlining relevant issues that Jones explored with a variety of sources representing Germany's business and political leaders. Additionally, it illustrates how Jones organized his raw notes into a cohesive report. Jones listened to von Schleicher's radio broadcast on December 15, and conducted numerous interviews on December 16 and December 17, the only dates recorded in the diary that he called "my few days in Cologne." Jones was a purposeful and diligent note-taker, evidenced in this pocket diary, and the notes served as rich veins of primary source material to incorporate into his report for Lee.

At the very top of the memorandum, Jones made a request for confidentiality. "I should be delighted if you show it to friends but some of those I interviewed did not want it to be quoted publicly." Jones noted whom he had interviewed, but asked that Lee not quote from his sources directly. "Since my stay was too short to make a real study of the situation and to draw conclusions for Germany as a whole, what follows is mainly a series of notes of conversations with a few observations."[40] Jones ended these introductory remarks by repeating his having visited Germany for ten consecutive years. One of those conversations was with a leader of the Christian Trade

42

Unions, named Kaiser, who explained his views about Schleicher and the working class. Jones recorded a direct quote in his notes.

> We had the impression that here was a man who understands the world of the worker. He especially understands our economic and social demands. We are ready for positive cooperation, but have no cause to attach ourselves definitely to this government.[41]

In the report, this becomes:

> Kaiser, the leader, said in a speech, that originally the Christian T.U.'s had mistrusted the new Chancellor but now he was known as "THE SOCIALLY MINDED GENERAL". The T. U.'s had the impression that here was a man who understood the working class. The Christian T. U.'s had a good impression of Schleicher as did the other T. U.'s, but their confidence would have to be gained by deeds.[42]

The most relevant part of the report was the section Jones titled, "The Decline of the Nazis: Prospect of Monarchy and the Growth of Communism," in which his sources predicted that the Nazis were unlikely to seize power, that Hitler was moving away from Socialism "in order that heavy industry may have confidence and enable the Nazis to pay their 12-million mark (£600,000) debt.... Personally, however, I think there is very little danger of a political revolt. The Reichswehr is too strong, the Communists are badly armed, and German Communists are the sort of people who parade in the very best clothes with clean collars and ties."[43]

Jones noted that Hindenburg on three separate occasions had opposed a Hitler dictatorship, and if Hindenburg died, the president of the Supreme Court of Justice would assume authority. He also was struck by an absence of panic. "The last time I was in Germany there were fears of a sudden catastrophe; now no one expressed these fears, in spite of the profound misery of the vast majority of the people."[44]

Unemployment remained the most pressing issue and Jones recorded several conversations with ordinary people he encountered as he moved from one interview to another. While he got information from officials like the Cologne Director for Poor Relief and the Director of Town Planning, Jones noted the concerns of a railway worker and "a man selling apples on station," who told him: "If I lost my job I'd have to live on 4/6 a week. Married man w/family gets about 12 marks a week. A friend of mine, an official, had to go on an expedition to search for weapons. Said that in one family children were eating potato peels."[45] Jones broke down in detail exactly what resources an unemployed worker could expect, what food, shelter, and fuel cost, and effects of poverty. "Many children cannot go to school because they have no shoes."[46]

That profound misery crystallized in calls for a large militia, an idea that was shared by Socialists and Nationalists alike. "I did not get the impression that there was a tremendous wave of militarism, but, of course, I was in Catholic Rhineland demilitarized Cologne, a very bad place to judge."[47] Jones was prescient in distinguishing the attitudes of Rhine-landers from other more militant Germans.

While it is not possible to know how impactful Jones's report was for Ivy Lee, it should be noted that at this time Lee began providing public relations advice to I. G. Farben [*Interessen Gemeninschaft Farben Industrie*] or the German Dye Trust, with worldwide subsidiaries. Lee had been retained by Farben's American subsidiary since 1929, but he now also advised the parent company, though stipulating that dissemination of information was beyond his purview.

When the Nazis came to power, Lee encountered problems related to messaging concerned with re-armament, growing violence against, and persecution of the Jews, and he counseled that any Nazi publicity deemed propagandistic would be regarded as meddling in American affairs. As one scholar of Lee has noted, there were contradictions in these attempts to assuage Americans that the Nazi government could be trusted. "It was all right to make radio speeches and write magazine articles, but they must not savor propaganda."[48] By the time Lee realized that he had made a mistake in assessing Nazi aims, he found himself and his records subpoenaed to appear before representatives of a Congressional committee investigating Communist and Fascist propaganda. Forced to justify his actions, Lee could not forestall the criticism that followed revelations of his activity.

'perfect bamboozling'

Jones did not publish an article based on the material gathered during this trip to Cologne until January 25, 1933, when the *Western Mail* published "The Sphinx of German Politics," a profile of the newly appointed Chancellor Kurt von Schleicher, who faced the daunting task of keeping Germany from being "torn by the bitterness of contending factions, of which the majority is seeking to shatter the existing system, and which has been long ravaged by hunger."[49]

Jones rounded out his feature by explaining that the name Schleicher meant "Creeper" or "Sneak", which characterized Schleicher's ability to outmanoeuvre his opposition by pulling the right strings behind the scenes. Describing him as the master schemer, Jones pointed to his "exceptionally broad views" and his desire to work with all classes as the reasons why "far greater confidence being placed in him by the German people than was placed in the hated Von Papen, who depended solely on a small clique of Monarchists." Despite being a military man, Schleicher, Jones reasoned, was "far more liberal and moderate than some of his fiery speeches and his arrogant military voice would indicate." Jones balanced that view by noting that Schleicher possessed the characteristics of a man of iron, "and he would not hesitate to act dictatorially."[50]

Jones's appraisal of General von Schleicher included a stinging rebuke of Hitler, who had demanded that Hindenburg appoint him chancellor.

> But the greatest triumph of his political cunning has been his complete outwitting of Hitler. In the whole of history there are few

THE SPHINX OF GERMAN POLITICS

By GARETH JONES

Von Schleicher, Master Tactician

A Western Mail article in which Jones suggested that Schleicher had got the better of Hitler. Five days later Hitler replaced Schleicher as Chancellor.

45

examples of such a perfect bamboozling of any leader as Schleicher's tactics towards Hitler. The miserable Nazi leader has been hindered and deceived at every step by Schleicher's superior manipulative skill. It is the capitulation of the loud-mouthed demagogue to the silent schemer.[51]

Jones's disdain for the "miserable Nazi leader" could not have been more clearly articulated, and Jones revealed a palpable disgust for Hitler, who had been utterly outmaneuvered by the Sphinx of German politics. Jones's estimation was based on events that transpired in the weeks following his return from Cologne, including Hitler's break with Gregor Strasser, one of his chief organizers, as well as the loss of support from Dr. Walter Pfrimer, leader of the Austrian National Socialists who withdrew command of his organization from Hitler. And after a dispute with Willy Stegmann, leader of the Franconian division of Stormtroopers who refused to execute orders, Hitler temporarily dismissed 12,000 Stormtroopers in Nuremburg.

Three days after Jones's article was published, however, Schleicher's tenure ended abruptly when Hindenburg refused to allow him to dissolve the Reichstag and Schleicher quit. When thousands of SA troops marched in front of DKP headquarters in Berlin, Hindenburg chose to keep the peace and appointed Hitler as the new chancellor. Jones, who was finalizing plans for his trips to Germany in February and the Soviet Union in March, could not have timed his trip more fortuitously. The assignment of a lifetime was about to become a reality.

Notes

1 Gareth Jones, "The Victim of 1930 – Familiar in Many Lands, *Western Mail*, December 31, 1930, 6.

2 Jones, "Victim of 1930," 6.

3 Jones, "Victim of 1930," 6.

4 Gareth Jones, Journal of a Tour of Germany, 1933, Gareth Vaughan Jones Papers, National Library of Wales, File B1/14.

46

5 Jones, "Victim of 1930," 6.

6 Jones, "Victim of 1930," 6.

7 Jones, "Victim of 1930," 6.

8 Jones, "Victim of 1930," 6.

9 See Colley, *More Than a Grain*, 95.

10 Gareth Jones, Letter dated January 2, 1931. Gareth Vaughan Jones Papers, National Library of Wales, File B6/3.

11 Gareth Jones, Diary – Europe and Russia, 1931, Gareth Vaughan Jones Papers, National Library of Wales, File B1/6.

12 Gareth Jones, "Poland's Foreign Relations," *The Contemporary Review*, July 1931, n.p.

13 Jones, "Poland's Foreign Relations," n.p.

14 Jones, "Poland's Foreign Relations," n.p.

15 Jones, "Poland's Foreign Relations," n.p.

16 Jones, "Poland's Foreign Relations," n.p.

17 Jones, "Poland's Foreign Relations," n.p.

18 Gareth Jones, "Fascist Dictatorship for Germany Now Possibility, Development," *New York American*, November 29, 1931, n.p.

19 Jones, "Fascist Dictatorship," n.p.

20 Jones, "Fascist Dictatorship," n.p.

21 Gareth Jones, "A Retrospective of the Banking Crisis," *Western Mail*, December 21, 1931, 6.

22 Jones, "A Retrospective," 6.

23 Jones, "A Retrospective," 6.

24 Ivy Lee, "Publication on War Debts & Gold Crisis," Address delivered at DePauw University, Greencastle, Indiana, February 21, 1932, n.p. Accessed from https://www.garethjones.org/american_articles/ivy_lee.htm.

25 Lee, "Publication on War Debts & Gold Crisis."

26 Lee, "Publication on War Debts & Gold Crisis."

27 Gareth Jones, Letter dated February 1932, Gareth Vaughan Jones Papers, National Library of Wales, File B6/4.

28 Gareth Jones, Letter dated March 4, 1932, Gareth Vaughan Jones Papers, National Library of Wales, File B6/4.

29 Gareth Jones, Letter dated May 24, 1932, Gareth Vaughan Jones Papers, National Library of Wales, File B6/4.

30 Gareth Jones, Letter dated July 11, 1932, Gareth Vaughan Jones Papers, National Library of Wales, Aberystwyth, File B6/4.

31 Will Wainewright, *Reporting on Hitler* (London: Biteback Press, 2017), 80-90.

32 Gareth Jones, Letter dated October 8, 1932, Gareth Vaughan Jones Papers, National Library of Wales, Aberystwyth, File B6/4. See also Reinhard Haferkorn, "Danzig and the Polish Corridor." *International Affairs* (Royal Institute of International Affairs 1931-1939) 12, no. 2 (1933): 224-239. Accessed 14 July 2020, doi:10.2307/2602567.

33 Gareth Jones, Letter dated September 14, 1932, Gareth Vaughan Jones Papers, National Library of Wales, Aberystwyth, File B6/4.

34 Gareth Jones, Russian Notes, 1933, Gareth Vaughan Jones Papers, National Library of Wales, Aberystwyth, File B3/14.

35 Gareth Jones, Appointment and Engagement Diary 1932, Gareth Vaughan Jones Papers, National Library of Wales, Aberystwyth, File B1/8.

36 Robert Skinner, Notes on a Conversation with Professor Samuel N. Harper, October 27, 1932. Despatch No. 871, State Department Archives, Living Conditions/550/861.5017. Accessed from https://www.fold3/image/68313029.

37 Gareth Jones, Letter dated September 13, 1932, Gareth Vaughan Jones Papers, National Library of Wales, Aberystwyth, File B6/4.

38 Gareth Jones, Letter dated October 8, 1932, Ivy Ledbetter Lee Papers, Seeley G. Mudd Manuscript Library, Princeton University, Box 2, Folder 27.

39 Gareth Jones, Gareth Jones, Letter dated December 4, 1932, Gareth Vaughan Jones Papers, National Library of Wales, Aberystwyth, File B6/4.

40 Gareth Jones, "Impressions of Germany," Memorandum, December 1932. Accessed from https://www.garethjones.org/german_articles/impressions1932.htm.

41 Gareth Jones, Impressions of Germany Diary, December 1932, Gareth Vaughan Jones Papers, National Library of Wales, Aberystwyth, File B3/12.

42 Jones, "Impressions."

43 Jones, "Impressions."

44 Jones, "Impressions."

45 Jones, Germany, December 1932.

46 Jones, "Impressions."

47 Jones, "Impressions."

48 Ray Eldon Hiebert, *Courtier to the Crowd: Ivy Lee and the Development of Public Relations in America* (New York: PR Museum Press, 2017), 410.

49 Gareth Jones, "The Sphinx of German Politics," *Western Mail*, January 25, 1933, 6.

50 Jones, "Sphinx," 6.

51 Jones, "Sphinx," 6.

3

Primitive Worship

'with Hitler over Europe'

Prior to departing on his journey, Jones worked out detailed travel plans while maintaining his position with Lloyd George, not realizing that within months he was to become the centerpiece of a controversy with worldwide implications. Having avoided the fate of millions and being able to choose from various employment opportunities, Jones opted for a position with the *Western Mail*. That he had multiple offers testified to his rare set of skills as a foreign affairs expert and journalist.

In a review of Jones's BBC talk titled "A Distant View: From Moscow," a *Daily Express* writer described him succinctly: "Mr. Gareth Jones is a typical young Liberal. That is to say, he is good-looking, dark, vivacious and equipped with a great facility for expression."[1] The anecdotes Jones told in Welsh that day satirized both Hitler and Stalin, and left little doubt about how Jones could use that great facility of expression. Despite having been offered a position with the BBC, Jones was decidedly against it, in part no doubt due to salary concerns. After his talk on the series "Wales from Abroad," Jones complained, "I think it is a disgrace to pay only 32 Guineas."[2]

Nonetheless, he had a clear idea of what he would have brought to the radio series. "The absence of democracy in Russia would make me think of democracy in Wales. My talk with Lenin's widow [Natasha Krupskaya] makes me think of education in Wales." When Jones opposed some plan, opportunity, or offer, however, he often leaked those feelings in his weekly letter to family. "I can only remember one or two Welshman I've met abroad and there's nothing exciting or interesting I can say about them. I've avoided British people in order to learn more about the country I'm in."[3] An unkind word in private correspondence was not unusual for Jones, especially if it served his purpose. And when Jones made his decision not to join the BBC, he noted: "B.[ernard] Pares thought I had done excellently in refusing the BBC and that it was a splendid idea to join the Western Mail."[4] In a postscript addressed to his Aunt Winnie, he wrote, "Ever since I heard that the Pennorth people thought I was like you I have become terribly conceited."[5] Jones's self-deprecation lent a touch of humor, despite his confessed assertion denigrating his countrymen.

In addition to good-natured self-deprecation, Jones often provided instructions about forwarding clippings of his published newspaper articles. He indulged in gossip; occasionally, he was the subject. Before leaving for Germany, he wrote this anecdote, which illustrates why Jones had such an integrated network of contacts:

> When the Captain's secretary had taken me to the Captain on board, she told a certain passenger (lady) that I was on board. "What! but I heard Mr. Gareth Jones give a wonderful lecture on Germany in New York." It was a German lady authoress who had spoken to me after I had lectured in the New York Town Hall Club. I met her in the train between Bremerhaven (the port) and Bremen (which is a 2 hours journey) and she seemed so excited to see me. She is well-known in Germany, middle-aged; and has asked me to visit her in Berlin.[6]

Coincidentally, Jones borrowed the BBC theme for his 12-part series he was hired to write for the *Western Mail* in February and April, titled "A Welshman Looks at Europe," covering trips to both Germany and the Soviet Union. What he had in mind was clear: Examine in detail the competing ideological experiments being conducted by the Soviet Union and Germany, Bolshevik Communism and National Socialism.

The die was cast on January 6, 1933, when Jones received his visa from Ivan Maisky, the Soviet Ambassador to Great Britain, who not only provided him with credentials but advice as well. "On Wednesday, I had caviar and a long talk alone for one hour with the Soviet Ambassador, His Excellency M. Maisky, a funny little chap, half-Tartar – half-Jewish looking, but who is a remarkably nice little fellow. He told me to wear warm clothes in Russia."[7] This letter to his family, as well as one to Lloyd George, specified that he was to visit Moscow and Ukraine, ostensibly to visit the Khar'kiv Tractor Factory as a guest of the German Consulate.

Jones mentioned to Lloyd George two recent Soviet Politburo resolutions: a food tax enacted January 15, and the assignment of the *Politodel*, special political section of the Communist Party, into the Machine Tractor Stations. What Jones did not know because it was by special decree, Stalin had issued an order on January 22 "to prevent the mass departure of peasants from the Northern Caucasus to other regions and entry into the region from Ukraine; ... to prevent the mass departure of peasants from Ukraine to other regions and entry to Ukraine from North Caucasus; ... to arrest peasants fleeing north from Ukraine and the Northern Caucasus and, after the filtration of counter-revolutionary elements, return the remainder to their places of residences."[8] By closing Ukraine's borders so that no food entered or left the region, Stalin effectively committed millions of people to starve to death. Stalin's order directed Vsevolod Balitsky, head of the NKVD in Ukraine, to round up peasants attempting to flee starvation conditions and return them to their villages to die.

In the days leading to his departure for Germany, Jones provided his family with early versions of his itinerary, which at this point in time had not been finalized, and personal news involving the Stewart family.

> Last night I took Margaret Stewart out to dinner. Ludovick [Stewart] is getting married in July. I'm paying all expenses for this journey myself. I remain a member of L.G.'s staff until the end of March but – *entre nous* – at a nominal salary. But it is worth everything to me to go to Germany as his secretary – it gives me wonderful entrée.[9]

> [...] I hope to sail on the S.S. Bremen a week Friday. Southampton to Bremen. Shall go to Bremen, Leipzig, Waldheim, Prague, Dresden, Berlin & Danzig, then Berlin. I have to return home for 2 lectures end of Feb. Then March 1st leave for Moscow – Kaluga – Kiev – stay a little in the Ukraine – then back home by the end of March. Splendid, isn't it. Don't be surprised when a big parcel (typewriter) arrives for me. Please leave it in my room.[10]

These two journeys brought Jones into direct contact with the beginning of Hitler's dictatorship and mass starvation in Ukraine, and that he had arranged it all so meticulously is perhaps why he characterized them as "splendid." Knowing he was about to witness extreme manifestations of Nazi and Bolshevik fanaticism, Jones armed himself with a new typewriter, a practical commitment to his newly chosen vocation.

As his departure date arrived, Jones provided instructions for correspondence, where specifically to reach him on given dates. "Mail to Rudolf Herzog, Leipzig...January 31, Paul Haferkorn; Waldheim go to mountains to ski. Then Dresden. Then to Danzig via Berlin, Feb. 9. Danzig Feb. 10-13 c/o Prof. Haferkorn, Danzig Free State. I have wonderful letters of introduction. It would be better only to send important cuttings to me. For the German addresses, write 2 days

A letter written at the Reform Club, in mid-January 1933, providing Jones's itinerary for his trips to Germany in February and the Soviet Union in March: "Splendid, isn't it".

earlier. For Danzig 3 days. Don't expect letters from Germany. I shall be working hard."[11]

'red light of alarm'

In February, Jones produced a 12-part series of articles for the *Western Mail* covering Hitler's appointment as Chancellor of Germany by Hindenburg. The overarching title of the series, "A Welshman Looks at Europe," contextualized the political and economic realities of Europe for the people of Wales. The main tropes used by Jones – the dangers of economic nationalism's dependence on tariffs and embargos, perceived injustices regarding war reparations, and the failures of the Treaty of Versailles – were completely in line with what Jones had been writing for Lloyd George and Ivy Lee. The December trip to Germany had only whetted his appetite to investigate more than what he learned from the Cologne interviews in December.

The *Western Mail* editors conceived of Jones's trip as comprised of two separate legs – through Germany on the first, and through the Soviet Union on the second. On February 6, the day before the series began, the *Western Mail* ran an article announcing that Gareth Jones was joining the newspaper's staff on April 1 and provided a biographical sketch delineating his many awards and accomplishments. On a separate page, the editors published a display advert announcing the series "A Welshman Looks at Europe". When the series about Germany reached its halfway point, the editors provided readers with a map of Jones's route. Jones corrected a slight error in that depiction in one of the letters he wrote between his stop-offs.

This series on Germany began by focusing on Wales's relationship with the countries of Europe. Titled "Wales's Bonds with the Continent," the first article, published on February 7, 1933, explained the key point – Wales and Europe were "inextricably bound. What is happening in Europe will hit or help Wales." Jones provided historical context by pointing to May 1931 as the day "the red light of alarm" was shone when Austria's greatest bank nearly failed, shattering the confidence of the world "that it led to the fall of the pound and had inestimable consequences to Welsh trade."[12]

Map showing Mr. Gareth Jones's travels in Central Europe on the tour he has been describing in the *Western Mail & South Wales News*.

The map published in the Western Mail on February 24, 1933, illustrating Jones's itinerary for his forthcoming "A Welshman Looks at Europe" series.

A Welshman Looks at Europe.

Mr. GARETH JONES
IS WRITING A SERIES OF ARTICLES ON THE SITUATION ON THE CONTINENT FOR THE

Western Mail
& South Wales News

THE FIRST WILL APPEAR TO-MORROW.

The advert, from February 6, 1933, the day before the Western Mail began publishing his series of articles on Nazi Germany.

Jones then brought focus to his journey by narrating his passage on a tender out to the SS *Bremen*, the world's fastest ship. They passed several anchored ships, idle, "a tragic commentary on the state of shipping." Jones found the Bremen almost empty. "Some of the officers curse the tariffs of the world, and one of them says, 'It is the doom of the white race which we are seeing now, and the yellow races are listening. Every nation is trying to save itself and basing its policy on a nationalism of a hundred years ago. Only a new outlook can rescue us."[13] The extent to which Jones agreed with his officer's assessment became clear in subsequent articles.

The second, published on February 8, defined the situation in Germany, as Jones created a man on the street scenario to express the popular slogans. "A crowd has gathered..." in front of a shop window with three photographs – one of Mussolini, another of a Nazi meeting in Danzig, and the third depicting "French soldiers dragging a German policeman through the streets of a German town." Not surprisingly, a German youth expressed the popular sentiment: "To think that we Germans have stood that disgrace for thirteen years! But we will stand it no longer. Hitler will bring us honour again." This rise of militarism in young people Jones knew lingered everywhere in Germany among Nationalists as well as Socialists. "Germany is bound to have a great army again, I thought, as the lights of Leipzig appeared and the train entered the largest station in Europe. What effect would that have on the peace of Europe and of Wales? The outlook seemed dark."[14]

'shrieking hatred'

Jones learned about Hitler's appointment as Chancellor while he was in Leipzig, and it served as the basis for his third article, "Hitler Is There, but Will He Stay?" Jones roamed the streets of Leipzig where he found all was normal. "I went to the station to look for any signs of revolt or of general strike. Nothing happened." When he attempted to purchase a Communist newspaper, he was told that newspaper had been banned. Jones found things "disappointingly calm... A few Nazi banners were hanging from windows in the Leipzig streets."[15]

Perhaps Jones was expecting a more boisterous response from the KPD and the trade unionists.

Jones outlined the problems Hitler faced in convincing German workers that he could make good his promise that "no unemployed man will be left in Germany at the end of four years." Because of many workers' deep disillusionment, Jones questioned whether or not Hitler could fend off the Communist Party. "If Hitler fails to banish misery and hunger many more millions will vote for the Communist Party, and the already nerve-stricken Germany will again be on the verge of civil war. In German politics, however, nothing can be prophesised."[16]

In the final section, Jones focused on Hitler. "The personality of Hitler arouses no confidence in the calm observer. It is hard to reconcile his shrieking hatred of the Jews with any balanced judgment. It is hard to think that a telegram he sent congratulating certain Nazis who had brutally murdered a Communist before the eyes of the murdered man's family reveals any spirit of justice."[17]

With this scathing indictment of Hitler's "shrieking hatred of the Jews," Jones made clear that Hitler and the Nazis had nothing in common with decency and justice. Having read *Mein Kampf* in German, Jones understood that the Aryan ideological core of National Socialism lay in hatred of the Jews, clearly articulated in the Nazi slogan – "*Der Jude ist an allem schuld*" [The Jew is to be blamed for everything][18]. Even though British sentiment tolerated much lower levels of antisemitism than in Germany, stereotyping of Jews was not uncommon. This impacted newspaper representation of the crisis, which tended to downplay Hitler's barbarism in favor of Germany's renewed confidence. As one journalism historian notes, "This limited the general sympathy felt for their plight, especially as few could envisage the depravity of Hitler's future actions against the Jewish population. Those who held serious concerns were invariably the same people who had taken the effort to read *Mein Kampf*."[19]

That Hitler had mounted another successful political campaign did nothing to assuage Jones's disdain for Nazi ends as well as the means to accomplish those ends. "Hitler's neurotic behaviour in a December meeting of Nazis, when he burst into tears and wept without control, was not that of a Bismark." The implication was clear: Despite having 13 million followers, Hitler exhibited none of the qualities a political leader needed to effect needed changes peacefully. In the final sentence, Jones offered another prediction. "If he fails to bring Work and Bread in Germany far more blood will flow in the streets of Berlin than has ever flowed before."[20]

Four days passed before the series continued in the *Western Mail*. During that time, Jones traveled to Waldheim, staying with Paul Haferkorn, with hopes to ski, but the rain ruined those plans. In the next four articles, Jones explored Bohemia, the Czechoslovakian countryside where he reported on the age-old problem of predation against minorities. Jones attempted to show that just as in Wales – with its two cultures and two languages – Germany and Czechoslovakia were embroiled in a conflict that had not been resolved by the League of Nations, a conflict known as the Problem of Minorities. "The nations in Europe which have the upper hand are trying to crush those members of their State who speak a foreign language. It is just as if the English did not allow any Welshman to have a responsible position, and as if the judges favoured the English in courts of law, nearly always giving judgment against the Welsh."[21]

Jones then explained how the German minority in Czechoslovakia had been unable to find justice. "By other methods, such as education and favouritism for non-Germans, by ejecting landowners and settling the land of the Germans by Czech or, in Poland, by Polish labourers, the dominant Slavonic races are attempting to crush their Teutonic subjects. The tables are turned. Formerly the Germans were ruthless in destroying Slavonic cultures. Now the hour of revenge for the Slavs has come."[22] Jones returned to this theme of minority rights in two 1934 articles.

The article elicited a letter critical of Jones, the writer of which pointed out that Czechs and Slovaks together comprised two-thirds of the total population and that Germans had ample facilities for education in their native tongue. "It is a travesty to say that 'the Czechs are now taking their revenge' and are oppressing the minority races." The writer also questioned Jones's assertion that law was used as a weapon. "There is every justice for a German in Czechoslovakia as indeed for any other national – perhaps even more justice in Czechoslovakia than for a German in Germany itself in these days."[23]

When his family pointed out that Jones had received several letters of criticism, Jones refused to temper his views. He wrote, "Please don't worry about correspondence in W. M. I am exceedingly glad when a controversy is roused. The Slovaks are exceedingly resentful against the Czechs but the Czech propaganda tries to show that everything is lovely. The Polish Press Bureau also tries to show that the Poles pamper the Germans!"[24] Jones certainly understood how the press could be manipulated into manufacturing content and contempt, depending what side had control.

The next two articles, datelined from "A Valley in Bohemia" and "A Village in the Ore Mountains, Czechoslovakia," explored folk culture. Jones used an ice break and home industries to frame the articles. The first he set in the village inn, "as the woodcutter and the toymakers were gathered ... singing their old folk-songs, a villager dashed in and shouted... 'The ice is breaking!'"[25] The innkeeper explained the dangers posed by the stream's blocks of ice that could take out a nearby bridge and damage homes downriver, necessitating a telephone call to alert them. Nothing compared with the disasters which the ice had brought 50 years ago, Jones was told.

In the second, Jones showed how woodcutters and toymakers were losing their livelihoods as a result of tariffs and mass production. Home industries suffered because of tariffs and "the spectre of the Machine." Their hardship became symbolic of a larger problem as greater mechanization threatened to eliminate craft labor. He recounted spending holidays as a schoolboy watching the village shoemaker, Robert Jones. "These men gloried in their craft. In the Europe of 1933 these men are disappearing, and their places are being taken by vast factories and vast companies, which are getting more and more a monopoly over the economic life of the world.... The Europe of 1933 is tariff mad."[26]

'into the camp of extremists'

Upon reaching Dresden, Jones focused specifically on German unemployed, at the time numbering more than six million workers. When looking into a shop window, Jones was approached by a young man who begged for money. As a farm laborers, the man received no unemployment insurance, driving "millions of honest German workers into the camp of the extremists. It is arousing among the middle class in Germany burning hatred of the system under which they live.... Unless the world hastens, however, to break down tariff walls to rescue Europe from the strangling grip of trade restrictions, and unless the mad militarists rampant throughout the globe calms down, the patience of the unemployed may come to an end and then woe betide Europe!"[27]

Jones described Germany's voluntary work camps, in which almost 300,000 young Germans were given work, bread, and health in the camps, similar to the labor camps Mussolini had created in Italy, and the Civilian Conservation Corps initiated by President Franklin Delano Roosevelt in the United States. Even the trade unions endorsed the measures, though Jones cautioned that "the Hitler Government wishes to make it compulsory and turn it into a kind of national conscription scheme."[28] Given that Jones had already emphasized the labor camps in the run-up to his journey, the articles do not provide much of any new information

Having arrived in Danzig, Jones communicated his satisfaction with the trip thus far, except for the quality of his articles. "I am thoroughly enjoying my trip to Germany. My visit to Dresden was a great success and I learnt a tremendous amount about the Voluntary Labour Camps.... It is very hard to find time to write articles. They have to be scribbled in odd times.... Wednesday, I came through Berlin. I went to see *The Times* correspondent, who, like myself, has little faith in Hitler.... I must spend as much time as possible in Germany, rush back, give the lectures and leave next day for Russia.[29] Interestingly, Jones was beginning to contemplate his journey to the Soviet Union, even though the most important leg of the German trip was still to come. The letter also reveals Jones's intention of returning to Berlin where he had arranged to have "about 30 to 40 conversations in Berlin with leading people. You remember my talking about the very nice Schulers in New York (Brooklyn). I shall be staying with them."[30] That his parents should remember who the Schulers were – people Jones met in New York City in 1931 whom he mentioned only briefly in correspondence – would be remarkable.

This transition from the stability of the Haferkorns, now paragons of the ideal married couple, to the quixotic Schulers and their religious and political connections warrants consideration. The relative arc

Eric Schuler and Gareth Jones in Prospect Park, Brooklyn, New York, February 1932.

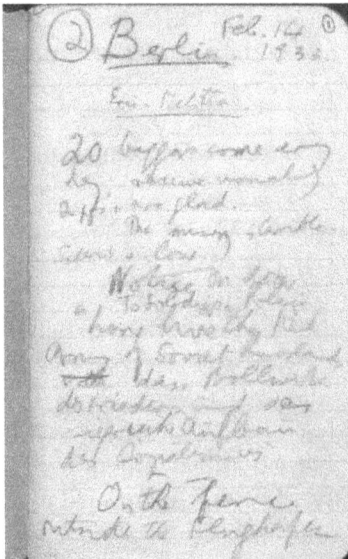

Jones's notebook entry, dated February 14, 1933, written in Berlin, which mentions the Schulers.

of this relationship between Jones and the Schulers takes on added significance given the events over the next several weeks entailing Jones's stay in Berlin through his journey to Khar'kiv, Ukraine, as a guest of the German Consulate.

Jones introduced Eric Schuler in a letter from October 1931: "Tonight I am taking Schuler (a very decent ex-German colonist in Russia) ... to dinner at my club."[31] Several weeks later, Jones mentioned that he was taking Russian lessons from Eric, who was out of work at that time. After a stroll in Palisades Park along the Hudson River and across the George Washington Bridge with them, Jones had to convince the couple to accept his dinner invitation as they had not been to a good restaurant for a year. The Russian language lessons continued until March 1932. On one visit after attending the Welsh chapel, Jones and the Schulers walked through Prospect Park in Brooklyn and took pictures.

The next time Jones mentioned the Schulers was almost a year later, February 5, 1933, in Berlin, Germany, when Jones provided his family an address to note and that he would be staying with "the Schulers (who were in New York; very nice)."[32] If that did not jog his family's memory, he provided an additional reminder a few days later, quoted above, and again in a

60

letter the following week. More importantly, Jones started a new pocket notebook once settled in Berlin, dated February 14, in which Jones took notes during the many conversations he had arranged in advance. Those appointments were scheduled over nine days, including one with Hitler's secretary. On the opening pages, however, Jones related an outing he took with the Schulers.

Eric & Melitta
20 beggars come every day; receive usually 2 pfs & are glad. The misery is terrible. Salaries v. low.
Notice on door – To Soldiers & Police
"Long Live the Red Army of Soviet Russland."
On the fence outside the airport: "Down with Imperialism. Long live Soviet Russia."
Walk
Hitler's cafe –
flag –

Melitta Schuler and Gareth Jones in Prospect Park, Brooklyn, New York, February 1932.

Eric. Three days ago at 1:30 in the night some communists came here with a car and threw a bomb into the window. It was probably a hand-made bomb because it exploded straight away. 3 men were wounded.

We saw window smashed & also the mark where a bullet had gone. Mayakovsky was killed in this neighborhood.[33]

The brief passage provides some evidence that conditions in Berlin remained tense. All indications suggest that the Schulers put Jones

A letter written in Berlin, dated March 3, 1933, in which Jones assured his family that the Schulers had "stocked me up with medicaments etc. & given me camphor against insects".

in touch with *Brüder in Not*, providing him with evidence of what was happening to German nationals in Soviet Russia. The Schulers also helped Jones get inoculated for his trip, "stocked me up with medicaments etc. & given me camphor against insects. As I told you, Eric Schuler is going to be collaborator. He has already done a tremendous amount of work and is already a happier man."[34]

The next mention occurred while Jones was in Khar'kiv on March 14 staying with the German Consul, "who is an uncle of Eric Schuler and who is remarkably kind to me. Tomorrow night we are all going to the opera to see 'Eugene Onegin' (Pushkin) and on Thursday, I shall travel with the German Consul-General on the wonderful train, the 'Arrow,' with sleeping car to Moscow, arriving there on Friday morning, 17th."[35] That the Schulers had an impact on Jones's journey to the Soviet Union is evident beyond dispute. What is not clear is what meaning should be inferred from the disparate facts, for the Schulers disappeared from Jones's correspondence almost as quickly as they surfaced. Jones saw them one last time in October 1934 when Melitta recounted a grizzly story. They returned to the United States and appeared on the 1940 census in Ithaca City, New York. By that time, they had a two-year old son named Gareth.

'disjointed'

The headline of the ninth article, "Storm over the Polish Corridor," used a double entendre to engage readers. Chronicling his flight back from Danzig to Berlin, Jones described the first storm as atmospheric, and it forced the aeroplane to make an emergency landing in Stolp after having flown 55 miles in 75 minutes. "The plane is rattling and shaking. There are more storm clouds in front. I am beginning to regret the excellent meal I took of pork cutlets and pancakes. The aeroplane has just recovered from a drop in the worst air-pocket I have ever experienced." Forced to spend the night in Stolp, Jones ended by connecting his delayed flight with a far more violent storm threatening the Polish Corridor. "When that storm of national passions will break no one knows, but the dark clouds are rapidly gathering."[36]

The metaphoric storm Jones

Letter in which Jones informed his family that he was giving Eric Schuler work "preparing my book on treaty of V[ersailles], Russia & and the L[eague] of N[ations]."

used to alert readers about the ongoing crisis between Germany and Poland over sovereignty of Danzig was more fully developed in a separate story published two days later. "The Red Light in East Europe," published on February 24, was not included in the "Welshman across Europe" series, though it provided a map of Jones's route, including part of his itinerary through the Soviet Union, Jones told his family the map was "a little wrong. I did not go to Austria."[37]

The editors at the *Western Mail* prefaced the article by explaining that Jones had the day before flown with Hitler to Frankfurt to attend a Nazi meeting, the result of a meeting Jones had with Hanfstaengl. "This was the first time Hitler had invited a foreign observer to fly with him since he became Chancellor."[38] While this was technically true, Jones was certainly not the first foreign journalist to accompany Nazi leadership to a rally, evidenced by the invitation Jones had

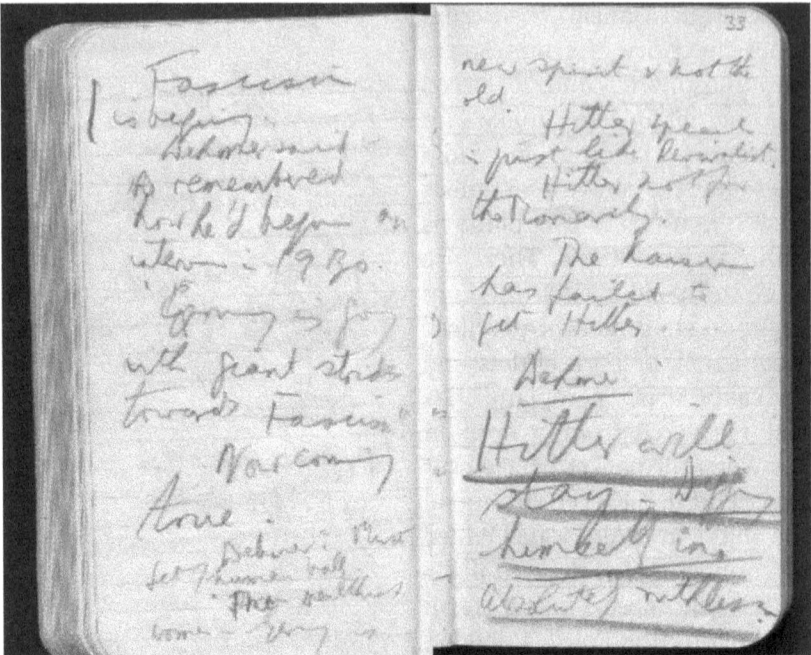

A notebook entry documenting the views of Sefton Delmer, the Daily Express journalist who was also on the flight to Frankfurt with Hitler and Goebbels.

received the previous summer, one that had been accepted by the other reporter on this flight, Sefton Delmer of the *Daily Express*.

It is noteworthy that Delmer chose not to memorialize this event in his memoir *Trail Sinister*. Delmer used the 1932 campaign to describe his experiences reporting on the prototypical Nazi rally as well as working with Hanfstaengl but never mentions this flight or Jones. For his part, Jones mentioned in his notebook that Delmer – who had ridden with Goebbels – had a camera and took "moving photographs" of Hitler's arrival and subsequent drive in Goebbels's new car, as the others waited. Jones noted, that one of Hitler's bodyguards "gives his photo as boxer to Delmer."

Throughout the journey, Delmer is cast by Jones as very much the senior reporter. During the flight to Frankfurt, which Jones noted reached a speed of 225 kilometres an hour at an altitude of 2200 metres, Delmer offered his political insights. "Germans have always been military. They'll act far quicker in Eastern parts than you think. They have the arms. Now clouds again."[39]

The Hitler section of that pocket notebook offers clues into Jones's practiced way of recording observations, data, and dialogue. The notebook's rendering of the flight is slightly more compacted than the newspaper article. "In Aeroplane over Berlin – Snow[.] If aeroplane should crash whole history of Germany would change." The page is marked with a large swastika with the name Hitler over it. This pocket notebook provides unvarnished experiences being recorded with some difficulty as Jones noted, "Difficult to write; consequently, in aeroplane, disjointed.... Huge aeroplane. Wings very long." At one point, Jones noted seeing what he thought was a curve in the river Elbe, using a question mark to serve as a reminder to find out; Jones later checked off that question mark by confirming their having flown over it. On one page, Jones showed Hitler and Goebbels, two monumental criminals, laughing at a joke in the newspaper, "nothing cold here; more Southern Bavarian." On another, they are planning "to clear away root and branch within four years all remains of International Marxist Policy in Germany." In making these raw notes, Jones was attempting to make sense of their banality, not their affability.

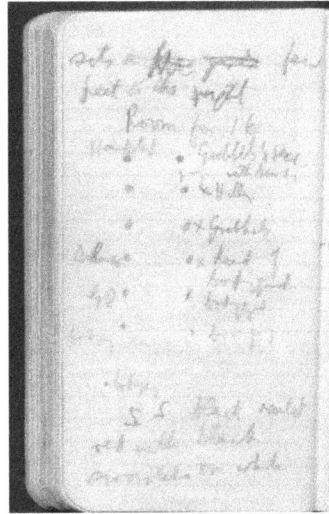

The seating arrangement for the flight to Frankfurt is noted. There was "Room for 16".

Sefton Delmer, who was an embedded journalist with Hitler during the 1932 election campaign, which led to criticism and claims he was a Nazi sympathizer.

65

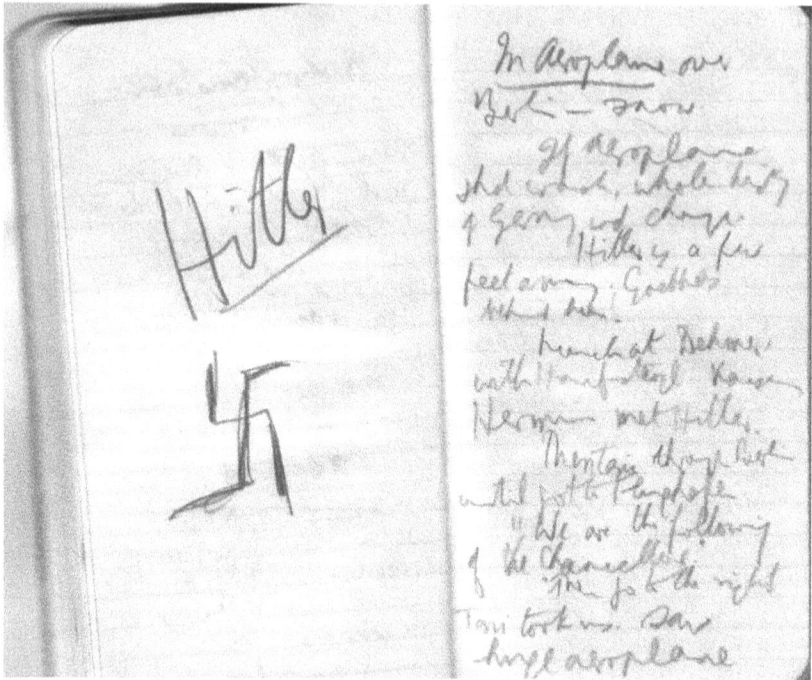

The notebook entry chronicling the flight with Hitler to Frankfurt, February 1933.

Jones underlined in thick pencil marks Delmer's warnings, knowing that he'd seen previous Nazi rallies.

> Delmer.
> Hitler will stay. Digging himself in & absolutely ruthless.
> Fascism is beginning. Delmer said: he remembered how he'd begun an interview in 1930. 'Germany is going with great strides towards Fascism.'
> Now coming true.
> Delmer: Worst set of human values. 'The wealthiest woman in Germany is tonight the unhappiest. Hermoine, the wife of the Kaiser has failed in her mission to convert Hitler to Monarchism.'
> Fascism is beginning. Talking to London. Mainly against Marxism.[40]

Jones later noted that his fellow correspondent was more careful in how he portrayed the Nazis in print than in conversation. In a letter, Jones wrote, "I have a feeling that Delmer did not write all he thought about Hitler. He probably wants to keep on the right side of the Nazis."[41] Having to navigate through the tidal ebbs and flows of repressive dictatorships was one of the difficult aspects of maintaining one's credibility, something with which Jones, Delmer, and others struggled.

Navigating the disjointedness of Jones's notebooks requires patience and a forensic detective's persistence, but they offer an unadulterated amalgam of uncut gems not found in the more composed newspaper articles.

'especially dangerous'

Jones doubtlessly paid homage to Delmer when he framed the first half of "The Red Light in East Europe" with a prediction; "one of the world's most renowned journalists made a remarkable prophecy to me, as we lunched in a restaurant just off *Unter den Linden*."[42] The only journalist besides Delmer that Jones mentioned in personal correspondence was *The Times* correspondent, whom he had met in Berlin on his way to Danzig. At the time, Norman Ebbutt served in that capacity, and like Jones, Ebbutt was very interested in the German church and provided ongoing coverage of changes affecting Christians living in Nazi Germany. But it seems clear, Jones was quoting Delmer when he characterized the prophecy of German troops marching across the Corridor to reunite East Prussia with Germany as alarming, though he well understood that millions of Germans "are facing eastwards."[43]

The article harkened back to the very first one in the series, revisiting many issues Jones had delineated about the Polish Corridor. The most salient concern was Germany's expansionist agenda. Jones explained that this had been confirmed by his visit to the Kaiserhof Hotel where he'd been entertained by Hitler's private secretary Ernst Hanfstaengl. "Of the several conversations I had with Nazis in the Kaiserhof one struck me as being especially dangerous

Hanfstaengl's signature on a letter to Gareth.

A Stars and Stripes photograph of Ernst Hanfstaengl, taken in Munich, 1957. Hanfstaengl had fled Nazi Germany in 1937. (Lloyd Borguss / © 1957 Stars and Stripes, All Rights Reserved)

in its implications in Eastern Europe. The Hitlerite said that Germany should look towards the East of Europe, where she should have economic and political power."[44] This observation by Jones proved especially prescient, long before Germany signed non-aggressions treaties with both Poland and the Soviet Union.

If Jones was struck by the possibility of Nazi expansionism, he was considerably less concerned when he described his time with Hanfstaengl to a letter to his family. "I went to see the Nazis on Friday at the Kaiserhof. I had 2 ¼ hours with Hitler's secretary – one of the funniest interviews I have ever had – he played marches on the piano and I sang nearly all the time. But must do a little more writing. I am thoroughly enjoying Germany this time. I always feel happy here."[45] That Jones so thoroughly enjoyed his time with Hitler's private secretary should not be dismissed as misguided self-aggrandizement. Delmer was even more enmeshed with Hanfstaengl, as he recounted in *Trail Sinister*.

> To get in with Hitler I had even hired a grand piano and installed it in my flat for Hanfstaengl to play, and I must admit it was always a treat to watch Putzi, even though I did get a little tired of listening to eternal repetitions of a march he had composed for the Stormtroops, the tune of which was in places remarkably reminiscent of *Mademoiselle of Armentieres*.[46]

A year later, in the article "The Hysteria of Goering," Jones admitted that he had been naively enthralled, in what he called "careless raptures", with the Nazis during this period. Events, including the Reichstag fire, the boycott of Jewish businesses, the opening of the Dachau concentration camp, and the Enabling Act, occurred while Jones was in the Soviet Union, making it more difficult for Jones to compartmentalize personal affinity in light of Nazi public policy.

'volcanic nationalist awakening'

Jones chronicled his flight with the new chancellor in "With Hitler across Germany," which begins with a memorable lede taken directly from his notes: "If this aeroplane should crash then the whole history of Europe would be changed. For a few feet away sits Adolf Hitler, Chancellor of Germany and leader of the most volcanic nationalist awakening which the world has seen."[47] Jones imagined the unimaginable, contextualizing the importance of the moment by invoking an extreme hypothetical. That scenario took on additional significance when considered against the backdrop of history over the next 12 years.

In this article, Jones characterized the collection of Nazis on the aeroplane as "a mass of human dynamite. I can see Hitler studying the map and then reading a number of blue reports. He does not look impressive." Jones described Hitler as, "a slight figure in a shapeless black hat, wearing a light mackintosh, and when he raised his arm flabbily to greet those who had assembled to see him, I was mystified."[48] Jones expressed bemusement about Hitler's boyish appearance. "Hitler is now turning and smiling to his adjutant [Brückner]. He looks mild. Can this be the ruthless enemy of Bolshevism? It puzzles me.... Hitler steps out of the aeroplane. But he is now spiritually transformed. His eyes have a certain fixed purpose. Here is a different Hitler. There are two Hitlers – the natural boyish Hitler, and the Hitler who is inspired by tremendous national force, a great Hitler. It is the second Hitler who has stirred Germany to an awakening."[49]

Much of the material for this story can be traced back to Jones's pocket notebook, including several items from *Der Angriff*, the newspaper started by Goebbels in 1927. One article that Jones jotted down previewed the meeting between Goebbels and Prince August Wilhelm for the following evening at the Sport Palace in Berlin. Jones recounted information "which I had picked up in Berlin. The Kaiserin had come to win over Hitler... Hitler kept the Empress [Hermoine] waiting in the drawing room twenty minutes while he chatted in the corridor outside ... and Hitler is not yet converted to Monarchism."[50]

Jones showed Goebbels reading Woodrow Wilson's Fourteen Points, a determined look on his face. No longer was he laughing at the joke Hitler had pointed out to him. "His smile has disappeared, and his chin is determined, he looks as if he were burning to avenge what the Nazis call the betrayal of 1918. I recall the Nazi slogan: 'Retribution.'"[51]

Lastly, Jones also recounted a story of Gerhard Schlemminger, who the previous day had been murdered by a Bolshevik. "This throws a light upon the political passions in Germany. I look again at Hitler. He and his followers feel that the hundreds of Nazis, such as this young boy who have died in street battles must be avenged, and they will be ruthless in crushing Communist opposition." [52] That Jones captured the contradictory nature of these Nazi leaders is evidenced in this important article, which illustrates how Jones crafted polished articles from spontaneous note-taking.

In the final two articles chronicling his trip to the Frankfurt rally, "Beginning of German Fascism," and "Primitive Worship of Hitler," Jones made clear that Hitler and the Nazis were taking actions that "have amounted to a *coup d'état* without violence."[53] Jones missed the mark with this statement, for while it was true that the Nazi ascension to power had not been a bloodbath, the British press had widely reported on the clashes between Nazi SA Brownshirts and KPD paramilitary.[54]

Jones certainly realized that simmering just beneath the surface was a misplaced enthusiasm fueled by a lust for power. "In a few weeks the Nazis have won the key positions, and they are not the kind of men to give them up. Goering has written a letter to the police which practically absolves them from any blame or responsibility if they shoot a Communist or a Socialist.... Law is thus rapidly becoming the tool of a party."[55]

In December 1932 Hitler had been roundly criticized in the foreign press when Herbert Hentzsch, a young Stormtrooper from Dresden, was murdered by three compatriots who subsequently fled to Italy to escape punishment at a time when Hitler was attempting to convince Hindenburg he could lead the nation.[56] For Jones, this Nazi disdain for responsible journalism was personified in the person of Goebbels, who was becoming more dictatorial in banning criticism, despite "his remarkably appealing personality, with a sense of humour and a keen brain."[57]

The architect of that public relations campaign was Goebbels, "the vivacious little man who sat behind Hitler in the aeroplane, and whose dark, narrow head and sharp brown eyes looked like those of a Glamorgan miner.... With the 'Herr Doktor,' as he is called, I have spent several hours." Jones was impressed by Goebbels's affability and keen intellect, but he also recognized another, more obvious, contradiction. "It is strange to think that this little man who looks so

Iberian, is a leader of the Nazi movement, which has as its basic the supremacy of the big, blonde Nordic race."[58] The description reveals Jones's ability to contextualize factual details into a larger portrait, one in which individual pieces did not necessarily mesh with the larger canvas. The Iberian-Aryan contrast masked the more sinister aspects of the Nazi propaganda minister.

'Herr Doktor'

The several hours Jones spent as the dinner guest of Goebbels after the rally in Frankfurt were documented in the same notebook diary as the flight and rally. Jones's diary notes in the Goebbels section emphasized the German return to militarism. "The League of Nations is dead. Hitler has killed it.... The rebirth of militarism in

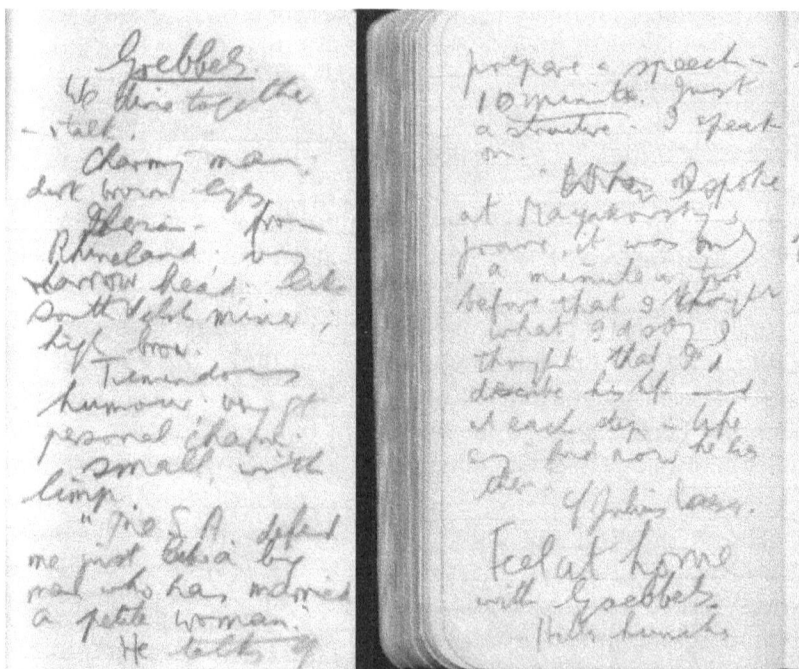

Jones's notes following his evening meal with Goebbels: "Feel at home with Goebbels".

Germany. <u>Militarism</u>. Goebbels and I drive to the station. He says, 'We'll stick to power. Nothing will get us out. From now on there'll only be Nazi ministers.'"[59] Jones noted that both Hitler and Goebbels extemporized during speeches, using a few notes scribbled on a piece of paper. Goebbels recounted for Jones his speech at Stormtrooper Mayakovsky's funeral. "'I thought that I'd describe his life at each step and say, 'And now he lies there.' c.f. Julius Caesar. Feel at home with Goebbels."[60]

This statement, recorded in the pocket notebook and published in the newspaper article, leaves a dark shadow across any portrait of Jones, who was taken in by the glib, erudite Herr Doktor's evocation of Shakespearean tragedy used to commemorate a fallen Nazi hero. Jones gave an indication as to why he felt at home with Goebbels when he noted, "I wonder if Goebbels takes things seriously; or is it more <u>self</u>-expression, love of fights, arguments. Argumentative. Can imagine him in discussions in S. Wales."[61] Jones related to verbal acuity, engendered in his family, nurtured in the Welsh Eisteddfod tradition, and honed under Lloyd George's tutelage. That Goebbels employed propaganda in *Der Angriff* to dehumanize Jews had not escaped Jones; that Jones overlooked this fact reveals a moral blind spot.

For his part, Goebbels recounted the meeting in his diary. *"Langes Parlaver mit dem Sekretar von Lloyd George. Ist zu Studienzwecken in Deutschland. Ein kluges Kopflein. Erzahlt schaurige Dinge von Sowjet-Rußland."* ["Long conversation with Lloyd George's Secretary. Is in Germany for study purposes. An intelligent young man. Tells me terrible things about Soviet Union."][62] Jones doubtlessly repeated that famine conditions were ravaging the Ukrainian countryside, exactly what he

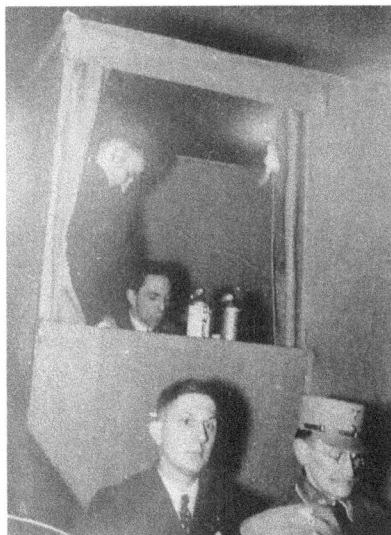

Goebbels in a broadcast booth during the Frankfurt rally.

73

had heard from Samuel N. Harper, Jules Menken, Sir Bernard Pares, and Bruce Hopper.

Jones concluded his profile of Nazi leadership by explaining how the Nazis had taken dictatorial control of all media, including print, radio (wireless), and film. The *Berliner Tageblatt*, which had been owned by a Jew and favored liberal politics, was closed almost as soon as Hitler came to power. "Responsible newspapers have been banned for criticisms. In this respect Germany is beginning to tread the path of Russia and Italy."[63]

Jones described Hitler's preparation for the rally by noting that Hitler and Goebbels jotted "a few slogans on two or three pieces of paper or outline a short plan and are usually carried away by the revivalist spirit." While the comparison was not particularly apt, Jones realized that he was "destined to witness one of the most overwhelming outbursts of national emotion which history records as the beginning of German Fascism."[64] Jones used foreshadowing to prepare readers for the next installment in the series.

'drunk with nationalism'

In his final piece for the series, "Primitive Worship of Hitler," Jones conveyed the affective emotions that gave the rally its defining quality, hysteria. Notably, Jones acquired a number of photographs taken at the rally by the propaganda ministry, providing visual documentation of the spectacle. One photograph of Hitler was taken from the dais only a few meters away. "I stand just a couple of feet away. Hitler waves his arm flabbily."[65] The photograph focuses on Hitler, flanked by a cadre of SA Brownshirts and SS Blackshirts, basking in the spotlight. Delmer had also described himself in this very position at an earlier Nazi rally in 1932. "I was up on the dais sitting on a hard chair with a huge swastika banner hanging down into this crowd that had been waiting for Hitler since the early morning."[66]

For independent journalists, finding themselves stationed not among spectators but on stage with Nazi leadership placed Jones and Delmer in a compromising position. Jones had neither the guidance, nor the journalistic experience to steer clear of questionable ethical practices. The extent to which his position as foreign affairs adviser allowed him this access should not be discounted, however, as the entire purpose of his reporting was to show the Nazi spectacle.

Jones summarized Hitler's speech by comparing it to the emotions of the National Eisteddfod, an important annual event that his Welsh readers easily understood. Jones drew a sharp contrast between the passion of the Eisteddfod and the Nazi political rally: "I have never seen such a mass of people; such a display of flags, up to the top of the high roof; such deafening roars. It is primitive, mass worship." Jones effectively captured the immediacy and frenzy of the audience, the deafening sounds of chanting. "The people are drunk with nationalism. It is hysteria."[67]

Jones was not terribly impressed with Hitler's speech. He noted, "Hitler begins in a calm, deep voice, which gets louder and louder, higher and higher. He loses his calmness and trembles in his excitement... Imagine a speech by Mr. Lloyd George. Take away the wit, take away the intellectual play, the gift of colour, the literary and Biblical allusions of the Welsh statesman. Add a louder voice, less varied in tone, a more unbroken stretch of emotional appeal, more demagogy, and you have Hitler."[68]

The rally, for Jones, was a clear manifestation of German Fascism, characterized by extreme fanaticism for the cult-like figure of Hitler. In a letter to his family, he noted, "The Hitler meeting was the most thrilling thing I have ever seen in my life – absolutely primitive.... I have spent a tremendous amount and must therefore save every penny when I come back. There won't be any trouble at all in Russia. Now I have to write some articles for the Financial News.... Don't send the Hitler articles to Russia."[69] These brief, seemingly disjointed phrases capture the accelerated pace of a compacted schedule that took him from Berlin to London to Liverpool to Surrey before his departure for Moscow.

'profound devotion'

The two-part piece Jones wrote for the *Financial News*, titled "Whither Germany?" and published on the first two days of March, chronicled events dating from Hitler's becoming Chancellor, his consolidation of power, and, in Jones's opinion, his moving towards dictatorship. Analytical in nature, the two articles outlined how the Nazis had seized power and were determined to keep it at all costs. It was the "force of the Defence Troops [*Schutzstaffel*] (SS men) and of the Storm Troops [*Sturmabteilung*] (SA men) numbering many hundreds of thousands of men, well trained in street fighting and moved by a profound devotion to their leader and to the national cause."[70] Jones warned that these troops had become a weapon meant to terrorize social democrats and communists, eventually denying them any rights.

Of greater interest to the readers of the *Financial News*, Jones reported that Nazi economic policy was drawn along ideological lines. "What their economic policy will be one has no inkling, except that an attempt will be made to introduce compulsory labour service, a move which will be hampered by financial difficulties."[71]

Jones used Goebbels's term "autarchy" to define Nazi enthusiasm for the economic principle which theorized "that each nation shall produce upon its own soil or in an area over which it rules everything which it needs for its economic existence."[72] Jones developed this idea by showing how Nazi economics were predicated on a coupling of foreign policy and trade. Exports necessarily played a minor role, "and it was, they maintain, a grave mistake for Germany to enter upon the field of world economy.... Following the line of this thought, Nazi economists claim that Germany must expand to the East, must follow the policy of colonizing Eastern Europe..."[73] as it had controlled in Medieval times.

Although the Polish Corridor was central to Germany's push eastward, Jones realized that any expansion had implications for the Baltic states, as well as Austria, Italy, Czechoslovakia, and those Soviet republics bordering Poland. "The National-Socialist hatred of Marxism need not extend to the Union of Socialist Republics, and while relations with Italy will grow warmer, there is no reason to suppose that there will be any new foreign political constellation."[74] Goebbels had told him that Germany must have a strong Baltic fleet. "It would be in Britain's interest to allow us to spread to the East. We hope to extend our *Macht* [power] & that then Poland will realize that it will be better to give back the Corridor."[75] It is clear that

Nazi expansionism was, in 1933, already an emerging theme that encouraged appeasement based on the premise a strong Germany would bring stability to a region decimated by the war and the Bolshevik Revolution.

Jones concluded the first piece by assessing Hitler's role in forming Germany's economic policies. Having the confidence of German businessmen, Hitler "will be strong enough to throw aside dogmas and theories when confronted with reality. In business circles there is little fear that the National-Socialists will attempt any unbalanced measures, and there is hope that they will succeed in restoring order and political quiet." Despite Hitler's purported steadying influence on Germany's continuously changing economic program, the enactment of a narrow agrarian tariff "will be difficult to undo and will have serious reactions upon industry and upon exports."[76]

The second part of the series, "The Clash between Industry and Agriculture," began with the opinions of Dr. Paul Bang, the State Secretary of the Reich's Economic Ministry, who opposed currency experiments. Orthodoxy in currency matters had led to improved industrial conditions, and Jones provided data from the Stock Exchange, unemployment figures, and the Stillhaltung Agreement.

Those favorable features of Germany's economic situation constituted only half of the story, and Jones then explained the difficulties confronting the entire country: a deficit of more than two billion marks, declining tax revenues, and a need to fulfill guarantees for agriculture, for exports to the Soviet Union, for shipping, banks, and other industries. Jones noted that the financial task facing the new regime was a gigantic one, and how the German government was to obtain funds to carry out the vast scheme of land settlement, or of compulsory labor service, was unknown. Exactly what role the government would play in industry was an additional problem.

Having outlined the major economic problems, Jones returned to what he considered the most dangerous struggle – between industry and agriculture, between a world economy or an autarchy. Jones again pointed to the increased tariffs on agricultural products as the defining move. "Their champion, Herr [Alfred] Hugenberg, has acted in the economic sphere with as much ruthlessness as Herr Goering has acted in the political sphere."[77] The tariff measure succeeded in alienating every one of Germany's best customers, while the

Soviet Union, Germany's greatest debtor country, faced increased difficulties.

Jones left little doubt about the prospects for this Nazi economic policy. "By Herr Hugenberg's intensification of tariff madness a severe blow is dealt to industry, which will lead to a reduced consumption of agricultural products, thus returning like a boomerang to hit the Agrarians. Costs of production will increase. Exports will be gravely impaired."[78] That Jones took dead aim at this policy should not surprise, as his preference for free trade was well established.

Having returned from Germany, Jones fulfilled his lecture engagements in Liverpool and Surrey, all the while preparing to leave for the Soviet Union. On March 1, he wrote, "What luck that the articles coincided with events in Germany.... German Embassy very impressed with my article. It was read to the Ambassador & considered 'very balanced and reasonable & unbiased.'"[79] That affirmation of his reporting by the German ambassador in Great Britain was important for Jones, and he would again make use of German hospitality as a guest of the German consulate in Khar'kiv, Ukraine SSR before announcing to the world that millions of Ukrainians were starving.

Notes

1 See Gareth Jones, Letter dated December 21, 1932, Gareth Vaughan Jones Papers, National Library of Wales, File B6/5.

2 Gareth Jones, Letter dated Thursday, January 19, 1933, Gareth Vaughan Jones Papers, National Library of Wales, File 14.

3 Gareth Jones, Letter dated Wednesday, January 18, 1933, Gareth Vaughan Jones Papers, National Library of Wales, File 14.

4 Gareth Jones, Letter dated Friday, January 20, 1933, Gareth Vaughan Jones Papers, National Library of Wales, File 14.

5 Gareth Jones, Letter dated January 23, 1933, Gareth Vaughan Jones Papers, National Library of Wales, File 14.

6 Gareth Jones, Letter dated Sunday, January 29, 1933, Gareth Vaughan Jones Papers, National Library of Wales, File 14.

7 Gareth Jones, Letter dated, January 6, 1933, Gareth Vaughan Jones Papers, National Library of Wales, File 14.

8 RGASPI, fond 558, list 11, file 45, sheets 108-109.

9 Gareth Jones, Letter dated January 27, 1933, Gareth Vaughan Jones Papers, National Library of Wales, File B6/5.

10 Gareth Jones, Letter dated January 19, 1933, Gareth Vaughan Jones Papers, National Library of Wales, File B6/5.

11 Gareth Jones, Letter dated January 25, 1933, Gareth Vaughan Jones Papers, National Library of Wales, File B6/5.

12 Gareth Jones, "Wales's Bonds with the Continent," *Western Mail*, February 7, 1933, 6.

13 Jones, "Wales's Bonds with the Continent," 6.

14 Gareth Jones, "Germany Wants a New Frederick the Great," *Western Mail*, February 8, 1933, 6.

15 Gareth Jones, "Hitler Is There, But Will He Stay?" *Western Mail*, February 9, 1933, 11.

16 Jones, "Hitler Is There," 11.

17 Jones, "Hitler Is There," 11.

18 See Lochner, *What About Germany?* 19.

19 Wainewright, *Reporting Hitler*, 125.

20 Jones, "Hitler Is There," 11.

21 Gareth Jones, "German and Slav: Century Old Problems of Minorities," *Western Mail*, February 13, 1933, 6.

22 Jones, "German and Slav," 6.

23 H. C. Gill, "Position of Minority Races in Czechoslovakia," *Western Mail*, February 23, 1933, 11.

24 Gareth Jones, Letter dated February 26, 1933, Gareth Vaughan Jones Papers, National Library of Wales, File 14.

25 Gareth Jones, "The Ice Breaks in the Mountains," *Western Mail*, February 15, 1933, 6.

26 Gareth Jones, "Home Industries on their Death-Bed," *Western Mail*, February 17, 1933, 11.

27 Gareth Jones, "Workless Millions of Germany," *Western Mail*, February 21, 1933, 8.

28 Gareth Jones, "How Germany Tackles Unemployment," *Western Mail*, February 21, 1933, 6.

29 Gareth Jones, Letter dated February 9, 1933, Gareth Vaughan Jones Papers, National Library of Wales, Aberystwyth, File 14.

30 Gareth Jones, Letter dated February 9, 1933.

31 Gareth Jones, Letter dated October 27, 1931, Gareth Vaughan Jones Papers, National Library of Wales, Aberystwyth, File B6/3.

32 Gareth Jones, Letter dated February 5, 1933, Gareth Vaughan Jones Papers, National Library of Wales, Aberystwyth, File 14.

33 Gareth Jones, Journal of a Tour of Germany, 1933, Gareth Vaughan Jones Papers, National Library of Wales, Aberystwyth, File B1/14.

34 Gareth Jones, Letter dated March 1, 1933, Gareth Vaughan Jones Papers, National Library of Wales, Aberystwyth, File 14.

35 Gareth Jones, Letter dated March 14, 1933, Gareth Vaughan Jones Papers, National Library of Wales, Aberystwyth, File 14.

36 Gareth Jones, "Storm over the Polish Corridor," *Western Mail*, February 22, 1933, 6.

37 Gareth Jones, Letter dated February 26, 1933. Gareth Vaughan Jones Papers, National Library of Wales, Aberystwyth, File 14.

38 Gareth Jones, "The Red Light in East Europe," *Western Mail*, February 24, 1933, 11.

39 Gareth Jones, Hitler Diary, 1933, Gareth Vaughan Jones Papers, National Library of Wales, Aberystwyth, File B1/9.

40 Jones, Hitler Diary, 1933.

41 Gareth Jones, Letter dated February 9, 1933. Gareth Vaughan Jones Papers, National Library of Wales, Aberystwyth, File 14.

42 Jones, "The Red Light in East Europe," 11.

43 Jones, "Red Light," 11.

44 Jones, "Red Light," 11.

45 Gareth Jones, Letter dated February 19, 1933. Gareth Vaughan Jones Papers, National Library of Wales, Aberystwyth, File 14.

46 Sefton Delmer, *Trail Sinister: An Autobiography* (London: Secker and Warburg, 1961), 142.

47 Gareth Jones, "With Hitler across Germany," *Western Mail*, February 28, 1933, 6.

48 Jones, "With Hitler across Germany," 6.

49 Jones, "With Hitler across Germany," 6.

50 Jones, Hitler Diary, 1933.

51 Jones, Hitler Diary, 1933.

52 Jones, Hitler Diary, 1933.

53 Gareth Jones, "Beginning of German Fascism," *Western Mail*, March 1, 1933, 8.

54 Wainewright, *Reporting on Hitler*, 86.

55 Jones, "German Fascism," 8.

56 "Insist Hitler Act in Murder of Nazi," *New York Times*, December 31, 1932, 5.

57 Jones, "Beginning of German Fascism," 8.

58 Jones, "Beginning of German Fascism," 8.

59 Jones, Hitler Diary, 1933.

60 Jones, Hitler Diary, 1933.

61 Jones, Hitler Diary, 1933.

62 Elke Fröhlich (Ed.) - *Die Tagebücher von Joseph Goebbels, Teil I* Register 1923–1941. [The Diaries of Joseph Goebbels, Volume 2/ Part III: Register, 1923-1941]. Accessed from https://www.garethjones.org/goebbels2/goebbels.htm.

63 Jones, "Beginning of German Fascism," 8.

64 Jones, "Beginning of German Fascism," 8.

65 Jones, Hitler Diary.

66 Delmer, *Trail Sinister*, 150.

67 Gareth Jones, "Primitive Worship of Hitler," *Western Mail*, March 2, 1933, 13.

68 Jones, "Primitive Worship," 13.

69 Gareth Jones, Letter dated February 26, 1933. Gareth Vaughan Jones Papers, National Library of Wales, Aberystwyth, File 14.

70 Gareth Jones, "Whither Germany? Hitler Moving towards Dictatorship," *The Financial News*, March 1, 1933, n.p.

71 Jones, "Hitler Moving," n.p.

72 Jones, "Hitler Moving," n.p. See also Jones, Hitler Diary.

73 Jones, "Hitler Moving," n.p.

74 Jones, "Hitler Moving," n.p.

75 Jones, Hitler Diary, 1933.

76 Jones, "Hitler Moving," n.p.

77 Gareth Jones, "Whither Germany? The Clash between Industry and Agriculture," *The Financial News*, March 2, 1933, n.p.

78 Jones, "The Clash," n.p.

79 Gareth Jones, Letter date March 1, 1933. Gareth Vaughan Jones Papers, National Library of Wales, Aberystwyth, File 14.

4

Deathblow to Democracy

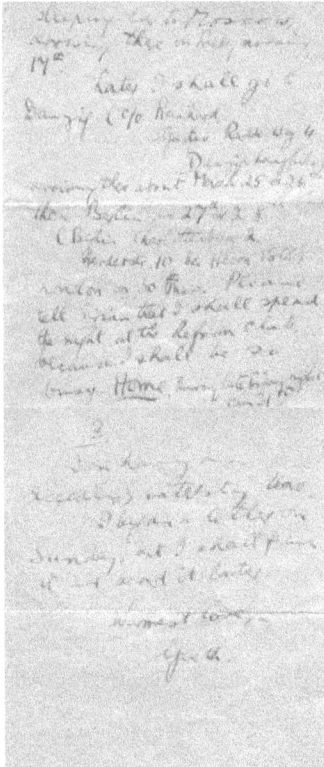

A letter written while in Khar'kiv describing his itinerary through to the end of his journey on March 31, 1933.

'such crass ignorance'

On March 30, following his return to Great Britain after completing his journey across Europe, Jones addressed the RIIA where he asserted that starvation conditions were ravaging the Soviet Union, and the next day published the article "Famine Rules Russia" in the *Evening Standard*. "I have never had two such days in my life. Yesterday the N.Y. Times, the Associated Press, the Allied Newspapers, the Press Association all wanted interviews!"[1] In his RIIA speech, Jones criticized George Bernard Shaw for a March 2 letter published in the *Manchester Guardian* in which Shaw and 20 co-signatories discredited newspaper reports about Soviet catastrophes. Having read the letter in *Izvestia* while in Moscow, Jones found it farcical. "Viewed from Moscow it was a mixture of hypocrisy, of gullibility and of such crass ignorance of the situation that the

RUSSIANS HUNGRY, BUT NOT STARVING

Deaths From Diseases Due to Malnutrition High, Yet the Soviet Is Entrenched.

LARGER CITIES HAVE FOOD

Ukraine, North Caucasus and Lower Volga Regions Suffer From Shortages.

KREMLIN'S 'DOOM' DENIED

Russians and Foreign Observers in Country See No Ground for Predictions of Disaster.

By WALTER DURANTY.
Special Cable to The New York Times.

MOSCOW, March 30.—In the middle of the diplomatic duel between Great Britain and the Soviet Union over the accused British engineers there appears from a British source a big scare story in the American press about famine in the Soviet Union, with "thousands already dead and millions menaced by death from starvation."

Its author is Gareth Jones, who is a former secretary to David Lloyd George and who recently spent three weeks in the Soviet Union and reached the conclusion that the country was "on the verge of a terrific smash," as he told the writer.

Saw No One Dying.

But to return to Mr. Jones. He told me there was virtually no bread in the villages he had visited and that the adults were haggard, gaunt and discouraged, but that he had seen no dead or dying animals or human beings.

I believed him because I knew it to be correct not only of some parts of the Ukraine but of sections of the North Caucasus and lower Volga regions and, for that matter, Kazakstan, where the attempt to change the stock-raising nomads of the type and the period of Abraham and Isaac into 1933 collective grain farmers has produced the most deplorable results.

It is all too true that the novelty and mismanagement of collective farming, plus the quite efficient conspiracy of Feodor M. Konar and his associates in agricultural commissariats, have made a mess of Soviet food production. [Konar was executed for sabotage.]

But—to put it brutally—you can't make an omelette without breaking eggs, and the Bolshevist leaders are just as indifferent to the casualties that may be involved in their drive toward socialization as any General during the World War who ordered a costly attack in order to show his superiors that he and his division possessed the proper soldierly spirit. In fact, the Bolsheviki are more indifferent because they are animated by fanatical conviction.

Friday, March 31, 1933   THE EVENING

FAMINE RULES RUSSIA

The 5-year Plan Has Killed the Bread Supply

By GARETH JONES

Mr. Jones is one of Mr. Lloyd George's private secretaries. He has just returned from an extensive tour on foot in Soviet Russia. He speaks Russian fluently—and here is the terrible story the peasants told him.

A FEW days ago I stood in a worker's cottage outside Moscow. A father and a son, the father a Russian skilled worker in a Moscow factory, and the son a member of the Young Communist League, stood glaring at one another.

The father, trembling with excitement, lost control of himself and shouted at his Communist son: "It's terrible now. We workers are starving. Look at Chelyabinsk, where I once worked. Disease there is carrying away numbers of us workers and the little food there is is uneatable. That is what you have done to our Mother Russia."

The son cried back: "But look at the giants of industry which we have built. Look at the new tractor works. Look at the Dnieprostroy. That construction has been worth suffering for."

"Construction indeed!" was the father's reply. "What's the use of construction when ..."

"The cattle have nearly all died. How can we feed the cattle when we have only fodder to eat ourselves?"

"And your horses?" was the question I asked in every village I visited. The horse is now a question of life and death, for without a horse how can one plough? And if one cannot plough, how can one sow for the next harvest? And if one cannot sow for the next harvest, then death is the only prospect in the future.

The reply spelled doom for most of the villages. The peasants said: "Most of our horses have died and we have so little fodder that the remaining ones are scraggy and ill."

If it is grave now and if millions are dying in the villages, as they are, for I did not visit a single village where many had not died, what will it be like in a month's time? The potatoes left are being counted one by one, but in so many homes the potatoes have long run out. The beet, once used as cattle fodder, may run out in many huts before the new food comes in June, July and August, and many have not even beet.

The situation is graver than in 1921, as all peasants stated emphatically. In that year ...

Jones's for the Evening Standard, published on March 31, 1933: "Famine Rules Russia".

Excerpts from Walter Duranty's New York Times article from March 31, 1933, in which he labeled Jones's reporting of famine as "a big scare story".

signatories should be ashamed of venturing to express an opinion about something which they know so little."[2]

Jones spent most of April completing the second half of his "A Welshman Looks at Europe" ten-part series for the *Western Mail*, commissioned alongside his seven-part series for the *Daily Express* and the three-part series for the *Financial News*. He had expected Lloyd George to summon him to report his findings about conditions in Germany and the Soviet Union, but that call never came. His revelations were being disputed by the communist press, which followed the lead of Water Duranty's denial in the *New York Times*. If Jones actually wanted to enter the pages of history with a vengeance, he accomplished his goal with considerable fortitude given the magnitude of the situation.

WESTERN MAIL & SOUTH WALES NEWS, WEDNESDAY, JUNE 7, 1933.

Germany Under Hitler—Third Article

CAMPAIGN OF HATRED AGAINST THE JEWS

NATIONAL LOSS IN TRADE AND INITIATIVE

By GARETH JONES

Jews are largely responsible for the decline in morals and for the corruption in public life. They state that the influx of Polish Jews has been damaging to Germany.

One day a leading Nazi said to me: "I tremble when I think of England. You are on the verge of a precipice and nothing but ruin awaits you. Do you know why?"

I waited for the reply, and it came: "You are doomed because of the Jews, who are working your downfall."

I almost rubbed my eyes. Here was a man of influence in the government of Germany, and he was talking in the terms of the Middle Ages. He continued in strains of fantastic ignorance, and his eyes sparkled as he enumerated the sins of the Jews. As I listened to him I felt as if I had been transported back many centuries, to an age of witchcraft and black magic, so unreal was his description of the so-called machinations of the Hebrew race.

When I got cut into the streets of Berlin I almost imagined that a pogrom might take place, so burning had been the

Indeed, Hitler looks upon the Bolshevik Revolution as a Jewish scheme to conquer the world, blissfully unaware of the fact that Lenin was no Jew, that Stalin is no Jew, that the most powerful Jews in the world are allied to capitalism, and that the Jewish shopkeeper, is the greatest sufferer in a proletarian revolution. But these little inconsistencies do not matter in the eyes of Nazis, for Nazis are quite capable of believing that Jewish Bolsheviks are working for the triumph of Jewish High Finance and that Jewish High Finance is subsidising a world revolution!

Even Jewish jokes are regarded by many Nazis as part of the subtle scheme of world domination by the Jews. Hitler suggests that the Jews try to depict themselves in comic newspapers as a harmless, humorous people in order to mislead public opinion into thinking that they are no danger.

The revolt against the Jews can finally be traced to the antagonism of the small shopkeeper to the fierce competition and unscrupulous methods of many of the larger Jewish concerns.

Thus the Nazis have dismissed Jewish doctors and lawyers, officials and professors. Even Jewish workers and employés have been thrown out to make way for men of German origin. In the realm of sport and art, science and education, the possession of Jewish blood is a barrier to progress.

What of the future? There are signs that the persecution is dying down, but that the damage done to Germany by it has been tremendous. Shakespeare wrote of the Jews: "If you wrong us, shall not we revenge?" and the revenge has come. Leipzig, the centre of the fur trade, has been dealt a severe blow. Germany's exports have suffered through a boycott of German goods. But the greatest loss to Germany, in my opinion, will be the loss in brains, in initiative, and in economic genius through which Jews enrich the countries where they live.

Headline of the third article in Jones's Western Mail series, "Germany Under Hitler".

That Jones returned to Germany by the end of May to write his next series of articles was doubtlessly motivated by the significant changes that had occurred in Germany in the interim. Those included the February 27 Reichstag Fire, the March 5 elections in which the Nazis garnered 44% of the vote and 288 seats in the Reichstag, the April 1 boycott of Jewish businesses, and the opening of Dachau concentration camp on March 22; most importantly, the Enabling Act of March 23 granted the Chancellor the power to enact laws without parliament's consent. Titled *Gesetz zur Behebung der Not von Volk und Reich* [Law to Remedy the Distress of People and Reich], this measure became the bulwark for the Nazification of German society. That same day Jones had interviewed Soviet Foreign Minister Maxim Litvinov in Moscow during which Litvinov shared views about Hitler's impact on the possibility for lasting peace in Europe. "I wonder whether Hitler is in position to control his forces or himself. He may bring about conflict with Poland."[3] The six-part series that Jones wrote about Hitler's consolidation of power was published in the *Western Mail* from June 5-10 under the umbrella title, "Germany under Hitler."

Hitler had used the plight of starving masses to bolster his election campaign against the social democrats and communists by lumping the two groups together as Marxists. Mass starvation in Ukraine became a discursive weapon Hitler used to rage against Marxist propaganda that workers in every nation would unite to destroy capitalist oppression. As Lochner noted, Hitler promised labor groups employment yet managed to assuage conservatives and monarchists by promoting Germany's rearmament. Before Jones had departed for the Soviet Union, Hitler addressed a rally at the Berlin *Sportpalast* in which he claimed that "millions of people are starving in a country that could be a breadbasket for a whole world."[4] This statement, along with those Jones had published the previous month, suggested that Hitler's expansionist agenda might include Ukraine as a source of wheat. It also left no doubt that Hitler had no need for Jones's reporting of mass starvation to make his condemnation of left-wing agrarian policies, but it doubtlessly reinforced that message.

Jones actively defended his articles about the Soviet Union as well as those of other journalists like Malcolm Muggeridge, responding with Letters to the Editor. For example, a few days after he responded to Duranty's denigration with a letter published in the *New York*

Times, Jones wrote in support of Muggeridge's three-part series in the *Manchester Guardian*. In the letter published on May 8, Jones not only confirmed Muggeridge's assertions of starvation, but he also directly appealed for international relief, providing the address for a German Evangelical organization, *Brüder in Not* [Brothers in Need]. Moreover, he directly rebutted criticisms that he and other journalists had lied.

> Attempts have been made in your columns to discredit the views of your correspondent. The "Moscow Daily News" has written on him an article entitled "When is a Lie not a Lie?" May I as a liberal-minded man who has devoted four years of university life to the study of the Russian language and history, and who visited about 20 different villages in the Ukraine, the Black Earth district and the Moscow region, as recently as March of this year, fully confirm his conclusions, and congratulate him on having been the first journalist to have informed Britain of the true situation of Russian agriculture?[5]

Identifying himself as an educated, liberal-minded man, Jones used his March journey through Ukrainian villages to confirm starvation conditions – children with swollen stomachs, no bread, no potatoes, no coarse beet, livestock dead or dying. "One phrase was repeated until it had a sad monotony in my mind, and that was: 'Vse Pukhili' ('all are swollen,' i.e. from Hunger), and one word was drummed into my memory by every talk. That word was 'golod' – i.e., 'hunger' or 'famine'."[6]

Jones quoted highly evocative descriptions from the letters that he had received from an Evangelical Church in Germany. In his plea, Jones advocated for international relief efforts and recognition for the victims. "I hope that fellow liberals who boil at any injustices in Germany or Italy or Poland will express just one word of sympathy with the millions of peasants who are victims of persecution and famine in the Soviet Union."[7] Jones made clear that raging against the injustices of bolshevism was as important as raging against fascism. Protecting religious freedom from persecution continued to be an important issue for Jones.

Having been the guest of the German Consul General in Khar'kiv, Karl Hermann Walther, Jones doubtlessly shared his impressions of conditions for the German colonists in Ukraine. Some of that information doubtlessly informed Walther's report to the Minister of Foreign Affairs in which he addressed the need for relief efforts.

> Recently, it was once again confirmed that the German Mennonites receive aid from their co-religionists in the USA and Canada on a much broader scale than German Lutherans, who are to be considered first in [the distribution] of aid.
>
> Regardless of the difficulties conditioned by the general situation and the particular "sensitivity" of the Soviet government, preventing the intensification of the propaganda effort in Germany and the aid campaign in the USSR – more should be done on the part of the Germans to aid our fellow men here.
>
> It should be undertaken to collect much larger sums than was the case thus far, with the help of the German Red Cross, church organizations and other, and as far as possible – together also with the official means.[8]

Walther's supplemental report provides documentary evidence that the German Ministry for Foreign Affairs was aware of deteriorating conditions for Germans in Ukraine SSR. Walther pointed out that death rates among Germans had increased, applications to emigrate had reached more than 200 in the month of May, and current levels of aid were insufficient. "In light of all this information, it must unfortunately be stated how little is known about the real situation of German colonists here.... I have recently learned of various cases in which the Soviet authorities attempt to stop German citizens from leaving, pointing to the alleged famine in Germany."[9] Jones would soon receive confirmation that his reporting of conditions had been accurate.

'I've become a journalist'

As with all of his trips abroad, Jones used personal correspondence to inform family and friends about his next planned trip to Germany and Danzig. For example, in a letter dated May 12 to Margaret

Stewart, Jones wrote that his goal was to focus on Hitler and what that ascension to power meant for Germans, for the Welsh, and for Europeans. The letter, which followed a postcard sent from Moscow on March 7, is worth quoting in full as it reveals a personal side to him beyond foreign affairs.

> My dear Margaret,
>
> Since the Cambridge train carried you off on that night in the end of January, all kinds of things have been happening, and I am wondering what you have been doing all the time. What is the summer term like and what about Easter?
>
> When is Ludovick [her brother] getting married? That'll be a great event.
>
> Next week I'm off to Berlin again and shall see what Hitler is trying to do.
>
> Do you know a family which would take a French girl this summer? She is 16 ½ and would like to give French lessons to a child or two and learn English at the same time; that is, *au pair*. Do you know anybody? Her name is Helene Roth and she lives in Colmar. She would be splendid and likes children; serious, I expect and very much of the *bien élevée*. I should be very grateful if you could help me.
>
> Please give my warm greetings to all at Girton Gate. [the Stewart home]
>
> This is a great life. I've become a journalist and it is wonderful fun.
>
> Best of luck this term,
> Love, Gareth[10]

From salutation to the train station departure to questions about Easter plans to the *entre nous* plea for help to satisfaction in having become a journalist, Jones's letter suggests a level of confidence beyond the ordinary. Jones had taken Stewart to dinner shortly before leaving for Germany in late January, even informing his family about it as well as information about Ludovick Stewart's marriage to Alice Naish in July. Jones had visited the Stewart family in late May 1932 when he and Ludovick accompanied sisters Margaret and Frida to a private dance. The friendship with Margaret can be traced back to 1930 when Ludovick, Jones, and Margaret, "and a friend

The Stewart siblings, right to left: Frida, Margaret, Ludovick, Katharine, and Jean.

called Joyce" dined at Naish's flat before going out "to the Circus in Olympia, which was excellent."

Although the biography mentioned that Jane Evans was the unannounced fiancé of Jones, Margaret Campbell Stewart (1912-2000), who returned Jones's letters to his family for the archives, appears on numerous occasions in letters and in his appointment diaries from 1930-1935. In addition to having been educated at Mrs Berry's Dame School. Margaret was enrolled at Newnham College, the women's constituent college at Cambridge University. As evidenced in Frida Stewart's memoir, Margaret and her sisters grew up in a very loving and supportive household. It is clear from Jones's letters that he had great confidence in Margaret and kept her apprised of his endeavors.[11] That she had the foresight to save his correspondence for posterity marks her as generous and prescient. Jones's relationship with the Stewart family provided Jones with loyal friends who shared love of language, literature, and the outdoors.

89

'wonderful picture'

By May 28, Jones was in Danzig, staying with Brigitte and Reinhard Haferkorn on election day where Jones learned that his reporting about the famine had been confirmed by the German Consul in Khar'kiv. In his letter to family, Jones conveyed what he had been told.

> German Consul in Kharkoff & his wife thought that my articles gave a wonderful picture that it is really <u>much</u> worse than I described. Since March it has got so much worse that it is horrible to be in Kharkoff, so many dying & all the beggars. They are dying off in the villages, he said, and the spring sowing campaign is catastrophic. The peasants have been eating the seed. To talk of a bumper harvest, as Molotoff did, was a tragic farce, and he only said that to keep up the spirits, but nobody believed Molotoff. Many villages are empty. The fate of the German colonists is terrible, in some villages 25% have died off and there will be more dying off until August.[12]

How Jones could use the phrase "wonderful picture" to describe his famine reporting is a legitimate question. The distinct counterpoint of "my articles gave a wonderful picture" against "it is <u>much</u> worse" resonates atonally whereby enthusiasm displaces empathy. It would sound less callous were he directly quoting the German Consul about his articles and giving more emphasis to the suffering.

Given the evocative descriptions of starving children Jones used in the *Guardian* letter and having visited the German Mennonites on all of his journeys to the Soviet Union, Jones knew firsthand the disastrous situation ravaging villages. He had received not only letters from *Brüder in Not* but also a press release stamped "*Nicht zur Veröffentlichung bestimmt*" [Not intended for publication]. Titled "*Bericht eines hervorragenden Suchkenners über die Lage in einem Teile des südlichen Sowjet-Russland im Frühjahr 1933*" ["Report of outstanding research over the situation in parts of southern Soviet Russia in the spring of the 1933"], the hand-typed document analyzes how starvation conditions impacted economic stability. The writer, like Jones, had found near-empty villages. "Depopulation is not only

90

increasing in the villages and areas affected by the resettlement and other political punitive measures, but is a general phenomenon in almost all the villages that I touched on the way."[13] [*Die Entvölkerung erstrecht sich aber nicht nurt auf die von der Aussiedlung und anderen politischen Strafmassnahmen betroffen Dörfer und Gegenden sondern ist eine allgemeine Erscheinung in fast allen Dörfern, die ich unterwegs berührte.*]

The German ambassador to the Soviet Union, however, had a distinctly different take on what the Ministry of Foreign Affairs should do in regards to conditions in Ukraine. In a June letter, Herbert von Dirksen contradicted Walther's assessment, pointing to favorable weather conditions that would likely result in a robust harvest in the fall of 1933, citing Dr. Otto Schiller's confirmation. More importantly, Dirksen echoed official British and American estimations that nothing should be done to alleviate the situation through international relief agencies. "I advise, according to the capabilities, stopping of the planned action – *Brüder in Not* – since at present it not only brings no benefits to the Germans in the USSR, but quite to the contrary, is harmful to them."[14] That the German ambassador and the German consul general had distinctly different perspectives on a course of action regarding international relief attests to the contradictory and conflicting reports emanating from the Soviet Union in the summer of 1933.

Not surprisingly, Jones also faced criticism from Welsh communists. When Jones's articles about the Soviet Union were challenged by Ithel Davies in *Y Cymro* [*The Welshman*], Jones readily responded, offering to pay Davies's expenses to travel to the Soviet Union. "If Russia is as successful as Mr. Davies implies, and making progress, why does Mr. Davies remain in Wales? Why does he not go to live there to see the nation's condition with his own eyes? I challenge him to leave his own country to live in Russia. I'm prepared to pay his travel expenses to Moscow on condition that he learns the language and stays there. Will he remain in Wales or will he go to Russia?"[15] ["*Os yw Rwsia mor llwyddiannus ag yr honna Mr. Davies, ac yn mynd ar gynnydd, paham yr erys Mr. Davies yng Nghymru? Paham nad aiff ef i fyw yno i weled gyda'i lygaid ei hunan sefyllfa'r wlad? Heriaf ef i adael ei wlad a mynd i fyw i Rwsia. Yr wyf yn barod i dalu ei dreiliau i Moscow ar yr amod y bydd yn dysgu'r iaith ac yn aros yno. A erys ef yng Nghymru neu a â ef i Rwsia?*]"

Jones also accused the *Western Mail* of using his articles to advance Tory interests, convinced that at least one of the letters was written by a professional journalist in a conservative propaganda office. "I am <u>not</u> going to be associated with Tories and Catholics of the W.M. type.... Everybody's views are doubted."[16] Being labeled a liar, Jones knew, was merely "the parrot cry" of the Soviet Government's supporters. In a similar way, Jones's reporting of Hitler came under attack from the British Union of Fascists, who saw in Hitler salvation and freedom from the oppression of poverty.

'revulsion of feeling'

In the first article of this series, "Germany Under the Rule of Hitler," Jones described in considerable detail how the Nazi Brownshirts had come to power behind Hitler for whom ordinary Germans had "a feeling which can only be described as that of religious worship."[17] Jones ranked the Nazi take-over of Germany with the Bolshevik Revolution in Russia and the Fascist *coup d'état* in Italy, though without the ravages of civil war and without delays. "They have dealt a deathblow to democracy in Germany, and have made Parliament into a despised relic of the past."[18]

Jones characterized the past as a series of failures and betrayals: failure of the Treaty of Versailles, limiting Germany's ability to recover; failure of the League of Nations to achieve disarmament; failure to stabilize currencies, failure to end embargos and tariffs; failure to forgive reparations; and failure to raise wheat prices by solving the wheat surplus. These failures had led to National Socialism's fanaticism, deeply rooted in hatred.

Jones pointed to dehumanization as the core principle of Nazi ideology. "They have started a ruthless campaign against the Jews, whom they have deprived of rights, whom they have persecuted both economically and morally, and whom they have treated as if they were 'inferior men,' as they call them. Distinguished scholars and great men, whom we in Britain would be honoured to consider as

92

citizens, are not allowed to enrich German scholarship or law courts or hospitals."[19]

That Jones pointed to this organized campaign against the Jews, begun officially on April 1, 1933, with a boycott of Jewish businesses, as the most conspicuous of Nazi blows against basic human rights and freedoms illustrated clearly Jones's contempt and outrage. Jones included in his list of other repressive measures: suppression of political parties, imprisonment of political, intellectual, and legal authorities, censorship of the press, and creation of a secret police.

Jones questioned what had precipitated these oppressive measures and then explained the years of unemployment, boredom, and alienation of Germany's youth that had poisoned their belief in capitalism. "Liberal-minded people have been shocked by the similarity which Nazi decrees have with former reactionary measures, and the treatment of the Jews has caused a revulsion of feeling which is shared by millions of Germans within the borders of Germany."[20] Jones certainly counted himself among those non-German, liberal-minded people, while publicizing the efforts of German Evangelicals.

Jones framed the article's conclusion by contrasting the stereotypical German values of cleanliness, orderliness, and efficiency with the abject poverty crying out for retribution. "This poverty is one of the forces which has made Hitler the dictator of Germany." As one scholar notes, this stereotype of the well-mannered, well-behaved Germany appears in Jones's work. In fact, once the Nazis had control of police force, many Jews, communists, and social democrats "were liable to be assaulted on the streets, to be beaten up, to be taken in and questioned, and this is going on all over Germany in broad daylight. Gareth doesn't actually report on that."[21]

That assessment is not completely accurate, for Jones overtly addressed the point of violence in the third article of this series.

> I have never seen a Jew struck, although there have been many cases of this, and visitors to Germany will be impressed by the outward decency of the towns. But often the quietest parts are the most ruthless battlefields, and so it is in Germany today, where the victims are not so much those who have been beaten in the streets or in the

Nazi Brown Houses, but those who have been dealt a death blow in the back by economic measures.[22]

This situation of not being witness to actual beatings was similar to Duranty's accusation that Jones had not himself seen anyone starve to death in Ukrainian villages. Jones, it can be argued, was indirectly addressing Duranty's criticism. The implication is clear: one need not to have witnessed individual incidents of violence against Jews to realize they were happening.

On at least two occasions Jones reported Nazi brutality and lawlessness. The first appeared in a February article "Beginning of German Fascism," in which Jones interviewed a member of the SS, who "was pointed out to me as a hero, for he had killed a Communist.... 'We set to. One of them came at me and I just took him up and crashed his skull against the piano. He was done for...'" For his crime, the SS man received amnesty. Jones included a lack of justice as part of Nazi tactics to terrorize and subdue. In the second account, Jones recorded a conversation with Otto Meissner Jr. concerning the arrest and execution of Karl Ernst, who along with 18 men were executed in August 1934 without a trial. Jones remarked in his notebook:

> Typical of the Germans was that a flower garden was in the spot where the men were to be shot. The S.S. men in the cars were anxious not to drive over the flowers, and took the utmost care that not a single flower should be trampled on. Then they shot 19 men.[23]

Jones used a macabre counterpoint to reveal the two sides of German evil: a meticulous care for flora and a distain for human life. Jones separated his affinity for German culture from manifestations of an ideology he despised, and he would be confronted with Nazi brutality right up to the very last days he spent in Germany when, in October 1934, he recorded in his diary Melitta Schuler's recounting about Idris Morgan's friend Gerda Sommer, who was callously murdered at the hands of Hitler's adjutant, Brückner. That Jones failed to condemn Nazi violence or only acknowledged what was happening without adequate condemnation does not withstand scrutiny.

'instinctive hatred'

In subsequent articles, Jones framed his portrait of Hitler as dictator by employing a variety of man-on-the-street ledes – "One day a leading Nazi said to me..." "I asked a German professor who had great experience in foreign travel, and who was a gentleman in every way..." "If you listen to the wireless..." "Before me I have a German book..." "I had not been many hours in Germany at the end of May..." They illustrate the immediacy and direct entry Jones relied on to bring focus to individual articles, as he had to manufacture interest in the individual piece while maintaining continuity in the series. The "Germany Under Hitler" series serves as an example of how he handled the complementary tasks. Jones combined the immediacy of a source's information "I am for Hitler because ..." with his own broader analysis:

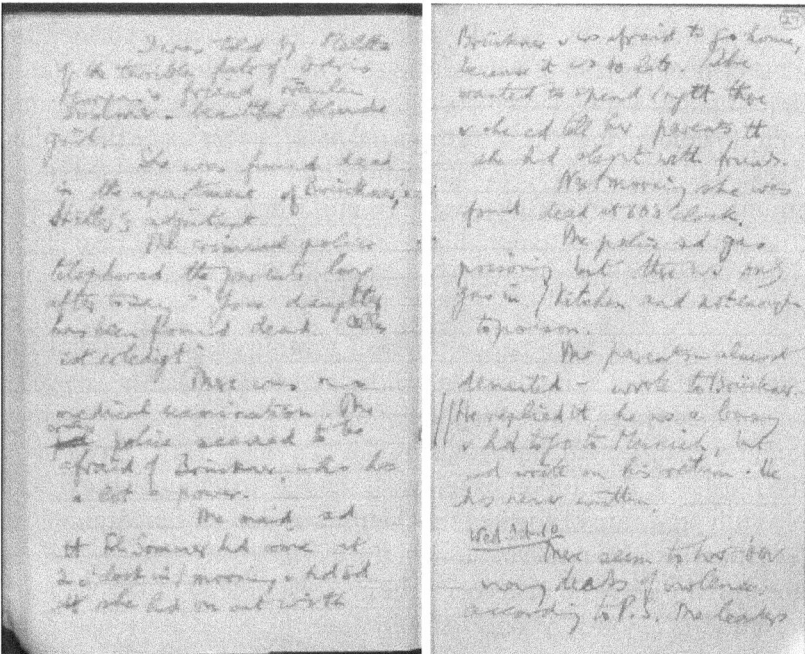

Notebook entries chronicling Melitta Schuler's story of Gerda Sommer's murder, October 1934.

Propelled entirely by deep feeling and by an instinctive hatred of self-government, the young Germans forgot some of the fine features of German democracy: its freedom of thought, its social services, and its housing schemes, and painted it as a corrupt Jewish invention to enslave the German people.[24]

Jones pointed to this accusatory trope of blaming the Jews for all Germany's problems as corruption, an attempt to enslave Germans by telling the biggest lies, creating a blind spot in Germans' articulations of the wrongs: the Treaty of Versailles, war debts and reparations, the War Guilt Clause, and the Polish Corridor. In throwing out the finer features of German democracy, millions of young Germans had grown up with the conviction "that they would willingly die on the battlefield to win back for Germany the Polish Corridor and other parts which they longed to see re-united to the Fatherland."[25] Jones felt that another war was a certainty, and he noted that sentiment in a movie poster he had seen in Berlin while walking with the Schulers.

In "Campaign of Hatred Against the Jews," Jones provided his most critical portrait of Nazi ideology. When a leading Nazi told him that England was doomed "because of the Jews who are working your downfall," Jones was transported back by "terms of the Middle Ages ... strains of fantastic ignorance, and his eyes sparkled as he enumerated the sins of the Jews."[26] So fantastical was this description that Jones confessed to imagining "that a pogrom might take place, so burning had been the hatred which the Nazis had expressed for the Jews."

Jones did not have to see physical brutality to understand the plight of the Jews. Having read Hitler's *Mein Kampf* [*My Struggle*], he outlined Hitler's entire argument against the Jews, showing how it had revived hateful antagonisms. For example, "Hitler looks upon the Bolshevik Revolution as a Jewish scheme to conquer the world, blissfully unaware of the fact that Lenin was no Jew, that Stalin is no Jew, that the most powerful Jews in the world are allied to capitalism, and that the Jewish shopkeeper is the greatest sufferer in a proletarian revolution."[27] Jones recognized fully that the Nazis were using the Jew-Bolshevik trope to demonize the Jewish population, and he certainly realized that antisemitism was tolerated in Great Britain, though not to the levels apparent in Germany. Nonetheless, the

THE NEW SALUTE

Herr Hitler's Breakaway—As the German Sees It . By GARETH JONES

"The New Salute": a cartoon published in the Western Mail on October 16, 1933, to accompany Jones's article, "Herr Hitler's Breakaway–As the German Sees It".

German public's turning a blind eye to this unchecked persecution had consequences beyond the immediate context of Hitler's attempt to restore German confidence.

This virulent campaign Jones attributed to a number of "the pettiest methods" to drum hatred of the Jews into the German people, including supremacy of the Aryan race, defense of Christianity, and the elimination of corruption and amorality. Significantly, Jones pointed to the Nazi revision of history.

> The worship of the Germanic past has led to an orgy of inventions about the history of Germany. The facts that the Germans are a

people of mixed origin and that the Slav element in the Prussian is exceedingly strong, are brushed aside scornfully, for Hitler has spoken and Hitler is always right.[28]

Jones explained how the Nazis dismissed Jewish doctors, lawyers, officials, and educators and replaced them with men of German origin. This travesty had accomplished nothing other than worsening the economy and diminishing education. "Germany's exports have suffered through a boycott of German goods. But the greatest loss to Germany ... will be the loss in brains, in initiative, and in economic genius through which Jews enrich the countries where they live."[29]

'four-note tune'

Jones used a direct address lede to begin "Worship of the Soldier under the Nazi Regime," in which he focused attention on the use of radio broadcasts to drum repeatedly a four-note tune. "If you listen to the wireless in Germany today, you will hear four notes being played time and again, and you find that it is the tune, 'People to Arms! People to Arms!'"[30] He reported seeing German veterans of World War I proudly displaying Iron Crosses in the cafés, and cinemas showing films of French soldiers about to execute the German officer who blew up a bridge in the Ruhr. Increased militarism was readily visible, Jones warned, best illustrated in the many uniforms and banners.

Jones recognized that German proaganda elevated the fallen into cult-like status worthy of emulation. This trope was used to "rouse the most passionate of nationalist feeling in the young Germans who see it, and makes them feel that they also would willingly lay down their lives as soldiers in the national cause."[31]

This cult of death, *Totenkult*, "can be traced all the way back to the death myth of World War I and is connected to such events as Schlageter's death destroying a bridge in the Ruhr, the saga of Horst Wessel, and, above all, the 'Immortals' of the abortive Hitler *putsch* on November 9, 1923."[32]

The Nazis used affect not only to commemorate martyrs but also to reinforce the idea of duty to nation above all else, which became an important theme of German *Bergfilm*. Mountaineering narratives showed intrepid explorers having to overcome obstacles through the concept of struggle – *"ein krankes Volk zu ertuchtigen"* [to educate a sick people] – and giving their lives to conquer unclimbed peaks.[33]

'heaven on earth'

More menacing than the failed German attempts to summit Nanga Parbat in the Himalayan mountains was a desire to grow Germany's army, exemplified in the abolition of class differences and barriers of inherited snobbishness that had characterized former German armies. "In the Brown Shirt Army, the sons of the Kaiser are in principle on the same footing as the raw peasant recruit."[34] However, as Jones explained, Hitler's foreign policy was unlike the Kaiser's, not to extend Germany's reach far abroad, but to make Germany "as independent of the world as possible. Towards the East! This meant in the long run war with Poland ... a profound danger to the peace of Europe in years to come."[35] Jones foresaw the next world war seeded in the misinformation, distortions, and lies of Nazi propaganda.

Jones decimated Nazi ideology by showing how it was a perverse form of organized religion in which Nazis were the true defenders of Christianity. Alfred Rosenberg had articulated the major ideas in his book *Myth of the Twentieth Century* in which, as Locher pointed out, the Nazi were negating Christianity in their *Weltanschauung*. Jones quoted from another book along the same lines, titled *Christianity in National-Socialism*, to show how ridiculous was the premise. "Since Christianity is, in Nazi eyes, a teaching which extols nationalism, it is the most patriotic of parties which is the most Christian.... By making everything German the Nazis are, in their view, carrying out the will of God!"[36] Jones took some solace in the fact that German protestants were not acceding to Nazi dictates about religion. "They have also shown that the Nazi interpretation of religion is not accepted by the mass of pious people in Germany, and that the idea of a military, patriotic Christ has not yet conquered over the gentler, nobler idea which inspires better Christians than the Nazis..."[37]

Jones, being a devout Welsh nonconformist, often explored the importance of religion in matters of politics. He exposed Nazi intolerance as decidedly un-Christian, not so different from the atheism of the Bolsheviks. Jones enumerated the points of similarities in his final part of the series, "Methods of Nazis, Fascists and Bolsheviks." Jones showed how dictatorships used religious scaffolding to support ideological ends. "The Hitlerites expect a new heaven on earth, just as the Bolsheviks are convinced that they will build up in Russia a paradise."[38]

Driven by the same kind of idealism, the Brownshirt and the Young Communist shared feelings of self-sacrifice, courage, and selflessness to secure complete power. Entrenchment was achieved with the formation of a secret police and the appointment of Nazis into the law courts whereby justice became a weapon of politics. "When a court of justice condemns a man to imprisonment for not giving the Hitler salute it can certainly be called a weapon of politics."[39] This would not be the last time Jones referred to the Hitler salute as a symbol of the Nazis' poisoned ecumenism. Equally important among the methods employed by all three dictatorships was the use of propaganda to mediatize German Nazification. All media were judged on a political criterion of loyalty to an orthodoxy that allowed no criticism. "Liberty of expression has also vanished and the careful guarded way in which Germans now talk makes one think of Moscow or of Rome."[40]

The worship of Hitler made Jones think of the worship of Lenin and Stalin by Soviets and of Mussolini by Italians, not surprising given the idea that the cult of the leader was a feature of these dictatorships. To conclude the series, Jones provided a final impression in which he reiterated the idea that Hitler had achieved his dictatorship without civil war, that Germany remained "remarkably calm," and that visitors would experience "the hospitality of a great people, who, in spite of their nationalistic views, give a warm and pleasant welcome to British guests."[41] Jones clearly defined himself as one of those guests, quite apart from his hosts like the Haferkorns, the Schulers, the Herzogs, and others with whom he had stayed and shared so much food, music, and conversation. Doubtlessly, he knew that these friends were aligning more closely with the Nazis, but secure within his own political and national beliefs, Jones was not inclined to follow.

Notes

1 Gareth Jones, Letter dated March 31, 1933. Gareth Vaughan Jones Papers, National Library of Wales, Aberystwyth, File 6/8.

2 Gareth Jones, Lecture titled "Soviet Russia in March 1933," Royal Institute of International Affairs, 30 March 1933. Gareth Vaughan Jones Papers, National Library of Wales, Aberystwyth, File A/4.

3 Gareth Jones, Diary of Tour of Russia, 1933, Diary 3. Gareth Vaughan Jones Papers, National Library of Wales, Aberystwyth, File B1/16. Transcription found in Lubomyr Luciuk, ed., *Tell Them We Are Starving – The 1933 Soviet Diaries of Gareth Jones* (Kingston, Ontario: Kashtan Press, 2015), 260.

4 Timothy Snyder, *Bloodlands – Europe between Hitler and Stalin* (New York: Basic Books, 2017), 61.

5 Gareth Jones, "The Peasants in Russia – Exhausted Supplies," *Manchester Guardian*, May 8, 1933, n.p. Accessed from https://www.garethjones.org/soviet_articles/peasants_in_russia.htm.

6 Jones, "The Peasants in Russia," n.p.

7 Jones, "The Peasants in Russia," n.p.

8 Karl Hermann Walther, Report by the German Consul General in Khar'kiv for the German MFA regarding the situation of German population in Ukraine SSR, June 16, 1933. Accessed from https://fayllar.org/poland-and-ukraine-in-the-1930s--1940s-unknown-documents-from.html?page=30#No._123__13_June_1933,_[Kharkiv]._Fragment_of_a_memorandum_by_an_employee__of_the_%E2%80%9CEast%E2%80%9D_Bureau_of_Section_II_of_the_Main_Staff_regarding_the_ever.

9 Walther, Report.

10 Gareth Jones, Letter dated May 12, 1933. Gareth Vaughan Jones Papers, National Library of Wales, File B6/5.

11 Gareth Jones, Appointment Diary for 1930, Gareth Vaughan Jones Papers, National Library of Wales, File B1/7. The entry for January 7, 1930, reads, "The evening was very enjoyable. I went to Alice Naish's flat and there met Ludovick, Margaret Stewart, and a friend called Joyce. After supper, we went to the Circus in Olympia, which was excellent." See also Letter dated May 30, 1932, in which mentions that Margaret was studying at Newnham. On that visit, he spoke with the eldest Stewart daughter, Jean Margaret, about her planned visit to the United States, and he traveled back to London with Frida, who became a communist, went to Spain during the Spanish civil war, and was imprisoned by the Nazis in France during World War II before escaping. See also postcard to Margaret dated March 7, 1933. "Heartiest greetings from Moscow to you all and best wishes for the Easter vacation. On Friday I go down South to Kharkoff, Ukraine. Europe is very exciting these days! Are you going away for Easter? What news of Ludovick? And how is your family?

With my best greetings also to Mr & Mrs Stewart and all, Gareth." Letter dated May 11, 1934. Gareth Vaughan Jones Papers, National Library of Wales, Aberystwyth, File B6/5. Postcard dated January 30, 1935. "I sail for Japan tonight & shall be about 6 mos. In Japan, Manchukuo & China, doing a series for the *Manchester Guardian & Berliner Tageblatt*." Gareth Vaughan Jones Papers, National Library of Wales, Aberystwyth, File B6/5.

12 Gareth Jones, Letter dated May 28, 1933. Gareth Vaughan Jones Papers, National Library of Wales, Aberystwyth, File B6/5.

13 Press Release, *Brüder in Not*. Accessed from https://www.garethjones.org/soviet_articles/bruder_in_not_1.htm.

14 Herbert von Dirksen, Letter dated June 16, 1933. Accessed from https://fayllar.org/poland-and-ukraine-in-the-1930s--1940s-unknown-documents-from.html?page=30#No._123__13_June_1933,_[Kharkiv]._Fragment_of_a_memorandum_by_an_employee__of_the_%E2%80%9CEast%E2%80%9D_Bureau_of_Section_II_of_the_Main_Staff_regarding_the_ever.

15 Gareth Jones, To the Editor of *Y Cymro* [*The Welshman*], September 16, 1933, n.p.

16 Gareth Jones, Letter dated October 25, 1932. Gareth Vaughan Jones Papers, National Library of Wales, Aberystwyth, File B6/4.

17 Gareth Jones, "Germany under the Rule of Hitler – Deathblow to Democracy," *Western Mail*, June 5, 1933, 9.

18 Jones, "Germany under the Rule," 9.

19 Jones, "Germany under the Rule," 9.

20 Jones, "Germany under the Rule," 9.

21 Dr Toby Thacker, qtd. in 'Germany, my Beloved Land,' *Planet*, 70-71.

22 Gareth Jones, "Campaign of Hatred Against the Jews," *Western Mail*, June 7, 1933, 9.

23 Gareth Jones, Journal of a tour of Germany, 1933. Gareth Vaughan Jones Papers, National Library of Wales, Aberystwyth, File B1/14.

24 Jones, "Germany under the Rule," 9.

25 Gareth Jones, "Germany Was Not Ready for Democracy," *Western Mail*, June 6, 1933, 9.

26 Gareth Jones, "Campaign of Hatred Against the Jews," *Western Mail*, June 7, 1933, 9.

27 Jones, "Campaign," 9.

28 Jones, "Campaign," 9.

29 Jones, "Campaign," 9.

30 Gareth Jones, "Worship of the Soldier under the Nazi Regime," *Western Mail*, June 8, 1933, 6.

31 Jones, "Worship of the Soldier," 6.

32 Harald Hobusch, "Rescuing German Alpine Tradition: Nanga Parbat and Its Visual Afterlife," *Journal of Sport History*, Vol. 29.1 (Summer 2002), 62.

33 Dr. Gustav Muller, "Die Berge und ihre Bedeutung fur den Wiederaufbau des deutchen Volkes," *Zeitschrift des Deutschen und Osterreichischen Alpenvereins* (ZDOAV) 53 (1922): 8.

34 Jones, "Worship of the Soldier," 6.

35 Jones, "Worship of the Soldier," 6.

36 Gareth Jones, "Nazis' Interpretation of Christianity," *Western Mail*, June 9, 1933, 11.

37 Jones, "Nazis' Interpretation," 11.

38 Gareth Jones, "Methods of Nazis, Fascists and Bolsheviks," *Western Mail*, June 10, 1933, 11.

39 Jones, "Methods," 11.

40 Jones, "Methods," 11.

41 Jones, "Methods," 11.

5

Riding the Nazi Tiger

'new hero'

Following Jones's series on Hitler's campaign to rid Germany of Jews, communists, and social democrats, Jones returned to his home town of Barry. His assignments for the *Western Mail* focused on unemployment and poverty in Wales, and more than a year would pass before Jones returned to Germany. That did not mean Jones ignored what was happening there, as he referred to initiatives and changes that resulted in Hitler's decision to abandon the League of Nations and sabotage the Disarmament Conference.

In an eight-part series titled "War on Unemployment," Jones contextualized the worldwide crisis of unemployment by focusing on Welsh poverty, especially in mining areas where unemployment benefits, health insurance, and improved infrastructure were acute needs. In these articles, Jones addressed the local measures being utilized to mitigate the effects of unemployment. Jones described the efforts of people like William Noble and others to create clubs that fostered the learning of new skills on a voluntary basis. "The new hero of Wales is now the unemployed man who has turned himself into a craftsman. ... One of the principles guiding the work is it shall not compete on unfair terms with men in ordinary employment. Only tasks are tackled which would otherwise be left undone."[1]

In subsequent articles, Jones used Germany's voluntary labor camps as an initiative that Wales needed to consider. "This voluntary labour service can be worked cheaply, providing the men with shelter, good food, companionship, and health in camps. It rescues these men from the apathy of worklessness, and when the moorlands are drained, homes are ready for the men where they can lead a hard, but healthy, farmer's life in the fields."[2] Jones warned that Hitler might "destroy its voluntary basis and make it compulsory and narrowly nationalistic."[3] Despite that warning, Jones admitted that Germany was years ahead of Wales in utilizing this type of program, but it remained a wonderful opportunity for the British Government to partner with clubs, town councils, and churches. "Wales has a chance of catching up to its brother nation and perhaps of beating Germany in the quality of work done."[4] Throughout the series, Jones showed Welsh workers needed infrastructure, not the desire or competence to accomplish tasks.

Jones sent a clipping of the article to Lloyd George, who responded by thanking him. "The notes from the Unemployed Camps are valuable. The papers here do not fully report Hitler's speech. What is it he definitely proposes to do and how? I am particularly anxious to know what his intentions are about the Land Settlement."[5] If Lloyd George cast Jones aside after his trips to Germany and the Soviet Union, it certainly was not apparent in this exchange. More importantly, Lloyd George's views came to embrace various Hitler initiatives. What has remained unclear was why

A letter to David Lloyd George, written in Berlin on March 27, 1933.

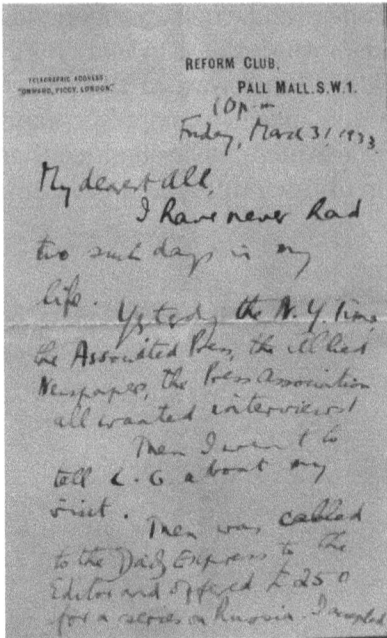

A letter to his family dated March 31, 1933. "I have never had two such days in my life".

Lloyd George never responded to Jones's letter of March 27 written from Danzig.

Part of the blackout can doubtlessly be attributed to a formal complaint the Soviets lodged to Lloyd George through Ambassador Maisky about Jones's reporting, which was an embarrassment compounded by Litvinov's having given Jones confidential information about the fate of the six Metropolitan-Vickers engineers accused of espionage. Additionally, Jones may have overstepped boundaries when he criticized Lloyd George's opinion of Stalin. "The situation is so grave, so much worse than in 1921 that I am amazed at your admiration for Stalin...."[6] Jones also noted that before his trip to the Soviet Union, he had visited Germany and met Hitler. "I made a special study of the Labour Camps, which impressed me deeply.... Therefore, I have much material on which you may want to question me."[7]

Whatever disappointment Jones felt when Lloyd George snubbed his offer, Jones transitioned into a full-time reporter for the *Western Mail* quite comfortably, ensconced at the house Jones had helped his family to purchase in 1932 during his tenure with Ivy Lee in New York City when the banking crisis made purchasing property a more solid investment.

Upon arriving in London for the World Economic Conference in mid-June, Jones sounded ebullient in sharing comradery with other reporters. "I have thoroughly enjoyed the Conference and met a number of journalist friends. It is great fun and I am exceedingly happy in my work. All the journalists like Dewall & Scheffer and Cummings are most kind. A. J. Cummings [*News Chronicle*] has the same picture as I have on Russia. He says that practically everybody is hungry, that the spring sowing is rotten, that there's not even enough food in Moscow or Leningrad & that the workers are undernourished. The outlook for the Conference is very black in practically everybody's opinion."[8]

Significantly, Jones appeared more interested in peoples' opinion about his articles on the Soviet Union than about those dealing with Hitler and Germany, though they were part of the same series. The number of times he mentioned his Soviet Union articles dwarfs the number of times he mentioned the Germany articles, as if he relished every mention as well as every invitation to lecture, to discuss over lunch, to debate what was happening in the Soviet Union. Despite following up the first series on Germany with a second, more scathing account of Hitler's dictatorial seizing of power with emphasis on the ruthless campaign against the Jews, Jones received only a few requests to speak about Nazi Germany.

'invisible forces'

On June 12, 1933, Jones reported from the World Economic Conference in London, and over the course of three days he wrote articles daily. Going into the sessions, the question Jones asked was whether or not the United States would recognize the Soviet Union. With Soviet and American delegations both negotiating, most believed recognition would follow this public rapprochement.

"Invisible Forces at the Conference" was the key article in which Jones portrayed the United States as desperate, "seething with discontent and misery."[9] Jones delineated the crises around the American failure to ratify the Treaty of Versailles and League of Nations. Recognition of the Soviet Union was a stated goal of the Franklin Delano Roosevelt administration, as well as solving the problem of falling wheat prices by negotiating an agreement among major grain-growing countries. The American desire to increase trade with the Soviets faced considerable obstacles from labor groups in the United States opposed to competing against forced or slave labor, as well as from non-political entities like the Catholic

Church, which vehemently opposed atheism and demanded that religious freedom be a pre-condition for recognition negotiations. Certainly, another obstacle to U.S. recognition of the Soviets was the Communist International's mission to work against capitalism through propaganda, trade unions, and workers' rights.

In order to establish a story frame enabling him to discuss "Conference Spirits," Jones used a scene from 1932 in which he and "an old negro preacher" watched children at play in a park in New York City. The preacher told Jones that the park was full of people, not only the living people, "but spirits, dem spirits is talking to us and guiding us, and dere are millions of dem floatin' about, and its dem what is important."[10] This awkward attempt at dialect was quite different from his description of a spiritualist meeting he experienced in a Harlem church in February 1932 when the Preacher pointed him out. "I see, Sir, that you have been to many spiritualist meetings and that you are deep in great study..."[11] Jones shared these experiences openly and presented this religious group as spiritual compatriots who welcomed him with dignity and a caring compassion. Jones recounted this episode in several conversations, so it certainly left an impression on him that he shared.

The first hovering spirit impacting the Economic Conference was the "American home-town man, or Middle West farmer ... who is now in misery"[12] and who blamed international banks and demanded payment of war debts. Poor American farmers had been laid low due to the unprecedented glut of wheat. Over several years, previous wheat conferences in Ottawa, Rome, and London had not achieved the desire of bolstering prices. Farm failures had decimated the small towns across the United States. Henry Wallace, the US Secretary of Agriculture, faced the daunting task of implementing the Agricultural Adjustment Act, which provided subsidies to producers of basic commodities for cutting their output. Even more difficult would be getting nations to agree on limiting acreage sown to stabilize the price of wheat.

The second hovering spirit was the spirit of vested interest, which worked to impose strict tariffs. "They exist in every country, but they are particularly strong this moment in America." The third hovering spirit was the dollar bill, the picture of Washington looming over millions of manufacturers and cotton growers and wheat growers longing to sell, despite a financial war between the pound and dollar.

The final set of spirits were the American politicians who had undermined their own president by defying Woodrow Wilson and his Fourteen Points, ultimately dooming ratification of the Treaty of Versailles. Jones criticized U.S. economic policy based on higher tariffs and predicted tragic consequences "when only international co-operation can save the world."[13] Nationalist economies were ruining all chances for recovery, a point Jones explored in the second article.

'wicked neighbors'

In "Greater Tariffs – Chief Question at the World Conference," Jones attempted to expose how the World Economic Conference took shape behind the scenes by comparing the Geological Museum to the grounds around an Eisteddfod pavilion where old friends greeted each other with familiar salutations. "It is in these corridors not in the conference hall that the news is to be found."[14] In the halls and corridors, journalists understood that what really spelled trouble for the conference was the rapidity of changes in America, nothing short of a revolution, according to Jones's source, an expert "who is not prone to exaggeration." Jones added commentary to what this American source told him.

> America's revolution has been almost ignored in this country, for it coincided with the far more spectacular advent of Hitlerism in Germany. But it is none the less true that Roosevelt is moving rapidly towards State planning and State control of industry. America's beloved "rugged individualism," which her leaders have vaunted so often, is dead and buried and an era of American Fascism seems to be on the horizon.[15]

Jones predicted that, before "this article comes into print," the U.S. Congress would pass the Industrial Recovery Act, putting the policy of economic nationalism into place and joining Germany and Italy in

109

adopting more quotas, embargoes, and tariffs. Jones concluded that the prospects for lowering tariffs were "exceedingly black".[16]

The big news that came out on the final day of the World Economic Conference was not that negotiators from the Soviet Union and the United States had actually sat at the same table, intimating that recognition was a distinct possibility. Rather, Jones used the Biblical allusion of David contesting Goliath to frame his article about Engelbert Dollfuss, the Austrian Chancellor, who gave a short speech about Austria's sound financial policy of a balanced budget to Conference attendees. Dollfuss quoted from a poem to challenge Hitler and Germany. "The best man cannot live in peace if his wicked neighbors cannot leave him in peace."[17] Jones explained that Dollfuss was defiant in the face of Nazi measures to prevent German tourists from crossing the border into Austria. Jones deftly punctuated the scene. "Dollfuss is hitting back with vigour and is stamping upon Hitlerism in his little country. As he was speaking, a German journalist whispered in my ear, 'The secret police have just arrested the Austrian Military Attaché in Berlin!'"[18]

Dewall and Scheffer were two German journalists with whom Jones was friendly, and he mentioned they both were covering the conference, so either may have been the source. However, in July, Dewall accompanied Jones on a tour of Wales, attending a debate Jones had in Merthyr at the Miners' Hall with Arthur Horner of Mardy. In a Letter to the Editor, Dewall praised the spirit of civility extended to Jones. "Such a debate could be held in no other country in the world.... The Merthyr audience struck me as exceedingly well conducted, keenly interested and intelligent.... They gave the critic of Communism a good hearing, and I was impressed by the fair-mindedness of the audience."[19] That Jones's criticisms of the Soviet Union were tolerated without incident pleasantly surprised Dewall, though Jones might also have shared tales of woe heaped upon unwelcome intruders.

Jones then transitioned to the speeches presented by U.S. Secretary of State Cordell Hull, Soviet Foreign Minister Maxim Litvinov, and former Prime Minister David Lloyd George. Jones characterized Hull's speech as an empty attack on economic nationalism undermined by refusing to address war debts. Litvinov was "mild and guarded" and whose rosy and unconvincing statistics belied the situation on the ground. Jones knew first hand that relations between Great Britain and the Soviet Union were dismal, given the British embargo on Soviet goods imposed after the conviction of two British engineers for espionage. Jones, who had visited Alan Monkhouse in Lubyanka Prison, decried the Soviet secret police for their treatment. Even though Litvinov was promising hundreds of millions in orders, Jones knew the Soviets depended on extended credit for exports and that those promises were received with considerable skepticism.

Lloyd George's speech focused on canceling reparations and war debts, which remained a sticking point, and he decried the use of tariffs and embargoes. Jones summarized the main points succinctly. Lloyd George "denounced the treatment of the Germans by the Allies. He could see the problem clearly. The answer was simply to cancel the Reparations and War Debts."[20]

Jones supported this position, and understood that the Conference would not solve the issues and antagonisms inherent in contrasting and competing ideologies. "The events of the Conference brought out clearly the rivalries in the world; the struggle between Austria and Germany behind Dollfuss's speech; the Anglo-American differences over dollars and debts, behind the speeches of Mr. Chamberlain and Secretary Hull; and behind M. Litvinov's words, the antagonism between two systems – Capitalism and Communism."[21]

'a young lady from Riga'

Soon after the conference ended, Jones reported on Nazi persecution of the German nationalists, former allies in the Hitler government, in an article headlined "The Nazi Tiger Claims New Prey." Jones enumerated previous prey – the Communists, the Jews, the Catholics, and now the Nationalists. Jones asked rhetorically why Nationalists were made to suffer when they had so much in common. "The truth is that there is no gratitude in politics and that the Nazis are swallowing up their Nationalist allies."[22] Jones used a simple limerick "There was a young lady from Riga / Who went for a ride on a tiger…" to illustrate how the "Nazi tiger" was coming back from the ride with a smile on its face, having feasted on its prey. For Jones, this betrayal proved that the way the Nazis seized power was no different from the Bolshevik Revolution. "Hitler is logically and ruthlessly pursuing his policy of uniting Germany under one control. He wants only Nazis to rule, only Nazi thought to prevail, and only Nazis to have leading posts."[23]

Jones was largely reiterating points he had made in both the February and June series. Even though Hitler had struck a conciliatory tone in his May speech regarding disarmament, Jones believed that Nazi worship of the soldier and the desire to expand to the East would, in years to come, lead to grave events.

> What of the Jews under Hitler? They are being treated as inferior beings. They are being boycotted. Many of the most brilliant among them cannot earn a living. The Jews are decidedly unhappy under Hitler!
>
> Then there are still perhaps 8,000,000 Socialists left in Germany. Many of them have lost their jobs, and thousands live in dread lest they should have to make way in office or factory for a less efficient Brownshirt. There are also those Socialists who are digging trenches and chopping wood in concentration camps. They are certainly not happy.
>
> Are liberal-minded men, internationalists, and pacifists happy under Hitler? Deprived of a living, unable to express their views, their novels banned, they are treated by the Nazis as enemies of the nation. ...
>
> Will Germany be happy, prosperous, and peaceful under Hitler? Many may be happy and peaceful for sometime to come. The Nazi ruling class may prosper for years. But I do not believe that any nation can long be happy, prosperous, or peaceful under a dictatorship which denies freedom, lauds militarism, and seeks to cut itself off from the rest of the world.[24]

Jones accurately foresaw that Hitler would first seize power, persecute the vulnerable, eliminate rivals, and ultimately break from the bounds imposed by foreign governments. That break came in the middle of October 1933 when Hitler took Germany out of the League of Nations.

As he had often done previously, Jones contextualized the break from a German's perspective by using a direct address lede. "Let us try to put ourselves in the place of the average German and interpret his feelings."[25] Jones recounted how Germans had stored in their memories "every little insult ... every slight ... until their supersensitiveness has produced the haughty, clumsy declaration breaking the bonds..." Jones recognized that national resentment was not the only cause for Hitler's decision. "Hitler will never forgive the Assembly of the League for the magnificent applause which greeted his enemy Dollfuss, nor will Dr. Goebbels forget the cold shoulders which showed him clearly how Hitlerism is hated. And it was in Geneva that Mr. Ormsby-Gore gave one of the most resounding slaps in the face which Hitler has ever had in a speech condemning the persecution of the Jews."[26]

Hitler had shown he would not tolerate criticism from the foreign press, evidenced by his threat to expel Soviet correspondents from *Izvestia* and TASS for complaining about an SA assault on Soviet journalists during the Reichstag fire trial in Leipzig a month before quitting the League. This belligerence was tempered by warnings from the industrial ministry that Germany was dependent on Soviet

A letter to his family, dated January 1933, shortly before Jones departed on his trip to Germany, with news about the Stewart family.

113

raw materials needed for rearmament. After warnings from Dirksen that rapprochement with the Soviets was better served with less tension, Hitler acceded in the short term; he also replaced Dirksen as ambassador in Moscow, sending him to Japan.

Jones showed that for all his rhetorical bluster, Hitler still had internal obstacles that banners, bands, and Brownshirts could not readily overcome, including not having enough bread, the disillusioned unemployed, and the specter of starvation. Having failed to solve the problems "of his desperate people from their empty cupboards and their tattered clothes," Hitler needed a distraction to maintain his popularity, so he created "some circus"[27] that would allow him to rearm Germany. The *Western Mail* added a political cartoon, "The New Salute," above Jones's article.

'choked with a surplus of wheat'

Jones was invariably drawn back into the battle of conflicting narratives about mass starvation in Ukraine. While more than 30 nations negotiated an agreement to prevent another collapse of the price of wheat – by restricting production – other organizations were making appeals to relieve the suffering of people starving to death. On August 19, Theodor Innitzer, Cardinal Archbishop of Vienna, issued an urgent appeal to the International Red Cross.

> Merely to look on such a situation would be to increase the responsibility of the whole civilized world for mass deaths in Russia. It would mean to bear the guilt of the fact that, at a time when whole sections of the world are almost choked with a surplus of wheat and food, men are starving in Russia.[28]

Innitzer's appeal appears similar to the report prepared by the German Consul General in Khar'kiv, and it may be that Innitzer was briefed on conditions sourced from Walther's report.

> In general it needs to be underlined that faced with the local system of moral pressure and oppression, it is difficult to prevent the

114

Bolshevisation of Soviet Germans, but a great majority of Soviet Germans continue to expect that the entire civilized world, and first of all the German nation, will spare no effort to save their lives and show all support in this difficult struggle. We continually receive requests to pay particular attention to their desperate situation, and it is impossible to understand why the entire world, and even the Fatherland, does so little to save them.[29]

Innitzer's appeal was directed not only to relief agencies, but also to all "those who are today negotiating for the enlargement of economic relations with Soviet Russia in order to make those negotiations dependent on the comprehension of the necessity for help in the stricken districts of that country."[30] The implication was clear and most obviously directed at the United States – make famine relief a condition for recognition of the Soviet Union.

The official Soviet response was published on the same page as the Innitzer appeal. The *New York Times* quoted a member of the Soviet Foreign Office: "There is no cannibalism and, I may say, there are no Cardinals in Soviet Russia."[31] The official called Innitzer's allegations of infanticide and cannibalism "pure fabrication..." and parroted Duranty's euphemisms about hunger and malnutrition but no famine.

The contours of the competing narratives about mass starvation were cemented in this reporting. Several years later, when Innitzer welcomed *Anschluss* and Nazi rule in Austria and raised his arm in the "Heil Hitler" salute, it provided an opportunity to question his motives in 1933 for international relief. Innitzer's purported appeasement of Hitler was called into question by Roman Catholic Church leaders in Rome, and he subsequently published a pastoral letter, "A Word to Catholic Parents," in defiance of Nazi education laws. Weeks later, Innitzer's residence was attacked, injuring him and his lawyer.

On August 30, 1933, the *Western Mail* published a story in which Innitzer's appeal was explained. Not surprisingly, Jones's eyewitness reporting of mass starvation was highlighted as part of the call for international relief. It was an obvious use of Jones's reporting of the famine by the newspaper to generate reader interest. "Striking confirmation of Mr. Gareth Jones's revelations in the *Western Mail &*

South Wales News of the famine conditions in Russia is provided by the Cardinal Archbishop of Vienna..."[32] In his appeal, Innitzer had cited several sources, but Jones was the only journalist.

> I draw your attention to the appeal of the Metropolitan (Archbishop) of Galicia, Andreas Scheptyckyj, who reports on the fearful sufferings of the population in the Ukrainian regions of the Soviet Union. The Englishman [sic] Gareth Jones also confirms this. Starvation in the Soviet Union is sweeping away members of all creeds and races. It is already certain that the catastrophe is continuing, even at the time of the new harvest.[33]

The *Western Mail* editors then made a most extraordinary confession: "Photographs of the famine-stricken population have been received in this office, but they are so appalling that no newspaper would venture to publish them. They show mass burials of victims of the famine and distorted bodies of starved children."[34]

These photographs were taken by Alexander Wienerberger and included in his book, *Hart auf hart. 15 Jahre Ingenieur in Sowjetrußland.*

Khar'kiv, August 1933. Corpses lying on the street photographed by Alexander Wienerberger.

Ein Tatsachenbericht [Hard on Hard: 15 Years as an Engineer in Soviet Russia, A Factual Report]. An Austrian engineer, Wienerberger had been taken prisoner by the Soviets during World War I and remained in the USSR, eventually helping build chemical plants. The photographs were taken while Wienerberger was in Khar'kiv. Wienerberger had provided a collection of his photographs to Innitzer, and it is likely those were the photographs the *Western Mail* received.

In its story, the *Western Mail* concluded with a reference to two people who had reported mass starvation. "The report of Dr. Schiller, agricultural expert at the German Embassy, Moscow, fully bears out the tragic conclusions of Dr. Ammende and of Mr. Gareth Jones."[35] Otto Schiller, a German agricultural attaché, had recently published a three-part series in the *Daily Telegraph*. Jones had met Schiller in late March outside of Moscow, and Schiller had confessed to Jones, "I am afraid that they may arrest me for sabotage. Horrible conditions in Central Asia."[36] Having traveled extensively across the Soviet Union, Schiller was experienced enough to know how to navigate through Soviet channels, so he obviously felt some pressure. Nonetheless, whatever information he provided Dirksen was ultimately used to stop relief efforts.

Having conducted several debates about conditions in the Soviet Union, Jones invariably became associated with Innitzer, Andreas Scheptyckyj, and Ewald Ammende, Secretary General of the European Nationalities Congress, who was an Estonian journalist, human rights activist, and politician of Baltic German origin. One diplomat in the British Foreign Office noted, "Muggeridge has no doubt that Dr. Ammende, whose protégé is Dr. Dietloff, is financed as an agitator by the German Ministry of Propaganda."[37]

That Jones could be associated with a purported agent of German propaganda has become the modern iteration of how to question Jones's reporting. The juxtaposition of Jones with the Nazis is convenient, even though no evidence has been found to show Jones ever met or worked with Ammende to write his articles for the Nazis, a point Muggeridge would certainly have confirmed.

Jones and Muggeridge each faced criticism for their reporting. In May, Jones had enlisted Muggeridge's assistance in countering Duranty's disparaging him in the *New York Times* at the very same time the Schiller articles were published in the *Daily Telegraph*.

Muggeridge promised to write the *New York Times* a letter of protest, but when Jones sent him a clipping of a Duranty story, he balked. "Thank you for your letter, and for the Duranty cutting. He just writes what they tell him to. At the same time, since his message refers to the new harvest I can't challenge him on first hand knowledge."[38]

Throughout the remainder of 1933, Jones continued to lecture and debate on both Soviet Union and Germany, revolutions which he had come to believe were much more similar, despite obvious ideological differences.

Notes

1 Gareth Jones, "Social Service War on Unemployment," *Western Mail*, April 25, 1933, 14.

2 Gareth Jones, "How Germany Is Helping the Workless," *Western Mail*, April 27, 1933, 11.

3 Jones, "How Germany Is Helping," 11.

4 Jones, "How Germany Is Helping," 11.

5 Gareth Jones, Letter dated May 3, 1933, Gareth Vaughan Jones Papers, National Library of Wales Library, Aberystwyth, File B6/5.

6 Gareth Jones, Letter dated March 27, 1933, Gareth Vaughan Jones Papers, National Library of Wales Library, Aberystwyth, File B6/5.

7 Jones, Letter dated March 27.

8 Gareth Jones, Letter dated June 11, 1933, Gareth Vaughan Jones Papers, National Library of Wales Library, Aberystwyth, File B6/5.

9 Gareth Jones, "Invisible Forces at the Conference," *Western Mail*, June 13, 1933, 7.

10 Jones, "Invisible Forces," 7.

11 Gareth Jones, Letter dated February 9, 1933, Gareth Vaughan Jones Papers, National Library of Wales, Aberystwyth, File B6/4.

12 Jones, "Invisible Forces," 7.

13 Jones, "Invisible Forces," 7.

14 Gareth Jones, "Greater Tariffs – Chief Question at the World Conference," *Western Mail*, June 14, 1933, 5.

15 Jones, "Greater Tariffs," 5.

16 Jones, "Greater Tariffs," 5.

17 Gareth Jones, "Britain's Policy Before the World Conference," *Western Mail*, June 15, 1933, 5.

18 Jones, "Britain's Policy," 5.

19 "German Journalist's Tribute to Audience," *Western Mail*, July 15, 1933, 7.

20 Jones, "Britain's Policy," 5

21 Jones, "Britain's Policy," 5.

22 Gareth Jones, "The Nazi Tiger Claims New Prey," *Western Mail*, June 23, 1933, 8.

23 Jones, "The Nazi Tiger," 3.

24 Gareth Jones, "Storm over Europe," *Western Mail*, July 15, 1933, 9.

25 Gareth Jones," Herr Hitler's Breakaway – As the German Sees It," *Western Mail*, October 16, 1933, 11.

26 Jones, "Herr Hitler's Breakaway," 11.

27 Jones, "Herr Hitler's Breakaway," 11.

28 "Cardinal Asks Aid in Russian Famine," *New York Times*, August 20, 1933, 3.

29 Walther, Letter date June 16, 1933.

30 "Cardinal Asks," 3.

31 "Moscow Official Issues Denial," *New York Times*, August 20, 1933, 3.

32 "The Famine in Russia," *Western Mail*, August 30, 1930, 6.

33 "The Famine in Russia," 6.

34 "The Famine in Russia," 6.

35 "The Famine in Russia," 6.

36 Gareth Jones, Diary of Tour of Russia, 1933, Diary 3. Gareth Vaughan Jones Papers, National Library of Wales, Aberystwyth, File B1/16. Transcription found in Lubomyr Luciuk, ed., *Tell Them We Are Starving – The 1933 Soviet Diaries of Gareth Jones* (Kingston, Ontario: Kashtan Press, 2015), 262.

37 Marco Carynnyk, Lubomyr Y. Luciuk, and Bohdan S. Kordan, eds., *The Foreign Office and the Great Famine of 1932-1933* (Kingston Ontario: The Limestone Press, 1988), 409.

38 Malcolm Muggeridge, Letter dated September 29, 1933. Gareth Vaughan Jones Papers, National Library of Wales, Aberystwyth, File B6/7.

6

Obstinately Unraised

'fantastic beliefs'

The new year began similarly to how 1933 ended. In mid-January, Jones delivered a speech, titled "The Germany of Hitler," outlining the changing conditions in Germany. As reported in the *Western Mail*, Jones told his audience that "Hitler had realized...that the national revolution had united Poland, France, Czechoslovakia, and even Russia against the menace of Germany.... The last few months, however, had shown Hitler the inadvisability of such a policy, and it was probably that he would follow the example of Mussolini in advocating peace rather than proclaiming the praise of war."[1]

Jones, like most of the foreign correspondents stationed in Berlin, believed Hitler had come to his senses after the antics displayed in Geneva where disarmament negotiations made little progress. By the end of the month Jones reported on the agreement Germany signed with Poland. In "Hatchet Is Buried for Ten Years," Jones characterized the "Pact of Understanding," signed in Berlin as a surprise, given the years of Polish hatred of Prussian repression and German demand for Danzig.

> It shows that Hitler has a sense of reality and a grasp of Germany's need for peace which few people would have expected of him. It shows that Germany's foreign policy is not to be based upon the hallucinations and glaring slogans of propagandist pamphlets, but on a sincere recognition that frontiers are frontiers, and that there

are other peoples in Europe than the Germans who want justice done to them.[2]

Surprisingly, Jones believed that this sudden deviation in course meant that Hitler had abandoned his ideology of hate for a foreign policy based on acceptance of territorial sovereignty. Referring to his 1931 trip to Upper Silesia, Jones reviewed relations covering the post-World War I period when parts of German territory had been given to Poland, noting Germans felt "humiliated at being ruled by a race whom they regarded as semi-Asiatic."[3]

Polish concerns stemmed from fears that Germany wanted Danzig. Jones pointed to "men like [Alfred] Rosenberg who advocated the expansion of Germany through the Ukraine towards the Black Sea."[4] This was not the last time Jones attacked Rosenberg, the minister of Germans abroad. Jones considered Nazi chauvinism an indication of aggression. In an article about the origins of the Eisteddfod, Jones again invoked Rosenberg to decry the creation of false idols and fictions about the Jews.

> Again, I think of how maddened I have felt in countries like Germany when men like Ludendorff have invented fantastic beliefs concerning Thor and Wotan and the ideal nature of the original Teutons, and when charlatans such as Rosenberg have spread pernicious forgeries about peoples like the Jews.[5]

Comparing the hatred of the Germans for the Poles with the centuries-old friction along the border between Wales and England, Jones asserted that despite the pact, the tensions along the frontier might erupt at any time. Sources had told him: "There might be a shot on the frontier at any moment which would set the Germans and the Poles killing each other as they did in 1921."[6] This passage was recontextualized into another article he wrote in May which summarized problems confronting the world, one of which remained Polish-German relations. "In spite of the signing of the German-Poland Pact, I hear from an expert who within the last fortnight talked with Reichswehr officers that military preparations on the German-Polish frontier are being carried on as vigorously as ever."[7] Jones often recycled material from previous interviews and articles to reinforce established points, especially when he could not travel and utilise notes generated from direct engagement.

'little Joneski'

Before Jones again ventured to the Continent to cover events in Germany, his interest in Soviet affairs was rekindled with the publication, in March 1934, of Malcolm Muggeridge's memoir, *Winter in Moscow*, which Jones reviewed for the *Western Mail*. Jones recounted meeting Muggeridge the previous March and heard from him stories of hunger and Red Army soldiers exiling thousands of villagers.

> At the time I thought that his disillusion in the Soviet Union had led him to exaggerate its darker features, but when, a few days later, I tramped through a number of Ukrainian villages, I realised that he had given a true picture, and that he alone of the foreign journalists in Moscow had had the courage to send to his newspaper a true account of the famine-stricken areas.[8]

Jones praised Muggeridge's book for its candor and courage in criticizing those personalities who failed to look beyond the Soviet veneer. Jones assured readers that Muggeridge, an avowed socialist, had not merely typecast people. "They are the real men and women who delude the world about Russia, and I can recognise them nearly all from personal knowledge. They will recognise themselves, too, when they read this book, and they will smart under Muggeridge's lashes."[9] Even though Muggeridge had failed to support Jones in repudiating Duranty's denigration, Jones was unwavering when confronting Western support for the Bolsheviks.

Criticism of the Soviet Union was also central to Jones's lecture to the Modern Language Association at University College, Aberystwyth, delivered in French. The news story's headline, "Britain through Russian Eyes," was misleading in that Jones used a single anecdote to show how the ordinary Russian, "nursed in profound ignorance," believed "the greatest power in Britain was Scotland Yard!"[10] Rather than security, the main topic of the lecture focused on "a dire scarcity of bread in the Soviet Union. Moscow was intentionally well fed, but in the country and in many towns, there was actual famine except for a brief period last year."[11]

Accounts published subsequent to Jones's journey the previous March had corroborated this assessment. The socialization of agriculture had disastrous results, especially the slaughter of livestock. The brutality of forced collectivization and dekulakization only exacerbated the suffering. Jones concluded his lecture by predicting that the change in Soviet policy to end indigenization [*korenizatsiia*] and to ban Ukrainian-language schools, publications and church services would result in war, "for rather than be forced to swallow high Russian the people of that province might appeal for help to neighbouring anti-Soviet Powers."[12]

Ever fascinated with life in Russia, Jones was pleasantly surprised when he learned that Margaret Stewart was considering visiting the Soviet Union later that summer. He responded to her news by offering to brief her on what to expect and by confiding exactly what had happened as a result of his journey there. This letter summarized in a most personal way the strange position in which Jones now found himself, feeling abandoned and apart those who had nurtured that fascination. Significantly, it also reveals his intention to travel to the Far East.

Dear Margaret,

Your summer trip to Russia sounds most exciting. The Caucasus is a thousand times more interesting than the Volga, which is grossly over-written.

It will be a job to evade Intourist and do it cheaply, unless you have someone with you who knows Russian. I am afraid that unless you're very lucky, Intourist will get hold of you.

One thing you might do is take your tickets through Intourist for the journey and for the first 2 or 3 days in Russia and then try and go off on your own. But it will be difficult and terribly expensive – unless you are wicked enough – as all journalists and diplomats are – to buy smuggled roubles on the Black Market (i.e., get about 250 roubles to the £ by illegal buying instead of the 7 roubles at the bank).

I do wish I could be in the region of Russia when you were about. Alas! you will be very amused to hear that inoffensive little Joneski has achieved the dignity of being a marked man on the black list of the O.G.P.U. and is barred from entering the Soviet Union. I hear that there is a long list of crimes which I have committed under name in the secret police file in Moscow, and funnily enough espionage is said to be among them.

So I have not the slightest relations with any of the people I know.

As a matter of fact Litvinoff sent a special cable from Moscow to the Soviet Embassy in London to tell them to make the strongest of complaints to Mr. Lloyd George about me.

I hope I can have a talk with you before you go. I have just come back from London where I have been fixing up a journey round the world, beginning in October. If I am up in London again, I might be able to come to Cambridge and talk your trip over.

Don't judge Russia from Moscow and try to go on your own to the villages which are real Russia.

I'm delighted to hear about Ludovick.

With my best greetings to everyone at Girton Gate and if there are exams this summer my warm wishes for success.

Ever sincerely,

Gareth[13]

Arguably, the most revealing of the many personal anecdotes Jones conveyed related to having not had relations with "any of the people I know." Despite numerous accolades from colleagues and friends, Jones found himself out of the loop, at least in terms of the Soviet Union. Having been in touch with Paul Scheffer on the eve of his departure for Moscow, Jones must have realized beforehand that if he reported mass starvation was ravaging Ukraine, he would be barred from ever re-entering the Soviet Union, as Scheffer himself had been. And he likely knew that the Canadian journalist Rhea Clymer had been expelled in September 1932 "for clearly defamatory, prevocational and completely fabricated information about the USSR" in her *Daily Express* reporting about "uprisings and hunger riots."[14] Jones had crossed the Soviets, using his status as Lloyd George's secretary to gain access, and then going public with confidential information about the Metro-Vickers engineers accused of espionage. In that respect, the decision to go public with the information confirmed his decision to become a full-time journalist.

Jones did not reveal to Stewart how he had learned about his secret police file and the accusation of espionage, though he did not take the charge completely seriously. The use of a Russified version of his name, Joneski, had first appeared in Jack Heinz's publication, *Experiences in Russia 1931 – A Diary*.[15] Heinz had also attended Cambridge University, though there's no known connection with the Stewarts. It is not completely clear what news about Ludovick that Margaret had told Jones, though in correspondence Jones expressed a soft spot for his friend. After meeting Ludovick at the Stewart home in 1932, Jones wrote, "Poor Ludo! He had a quarrel with the headmaster at Uppingham and has now a post in Manchester Grammar School. I expect his discipline was bad, because Ludo has no self confidence."[16] Ludovick had married Alice Naish the previous summer, which Jones doubtlessly knew, having inquired about her older brother's impending marriage in previous letters and postcards.

That he encouraged Margaret to get better exchange rates on the black market by avoiding the banks was not surprising given that on every trip he had taken there, he documented run-ins with the authorities in which he escaped unscathed. Those run-ins included boarding a tram without a ticket or change to pay for it, being threatened with a fine for boarding a train with Heinz without a ticket, and brazenly confronting a Communist Party member's assertion that there was no famine by throwing a crust of bread and an orange peel in a spittoon and having it immediately grabbed and eaten.[17]

Revealing that he was already formulating plans to go round the world by heading west across the United States to the Far East, Jones was perhaps looking for someone to give him a reason not to go. Not having Stewart's letters blinds researchers to her point of view. To what extent this new trip would reinvigorate his career as a foreign affairs correspondent is not entirely clear, but it's difficult to imagine that those closest to him would have been pleased. As he had done for previous journeys, Jones lined up newspapers willing to take his work, and the details of his plans and what he would be earning were spelled out in numerous letters to family and friends.

"blackening the skies"

Before embarking on that journey, Jones returned to Germany in June 1934 from where he wrote two articles chronicling the development of Germany's air force, and the murder of Ernst Röehm and purging of the SA Brownshirts. After attending a speech by Goering in his capacity as Air Minister, Jones wrote "10,000 Planes on German Frontiers," in which he described Germany's greatest ambition "to lead the world in civil and military aviation."[18] He also recounted his flight with Hitler back in February and Germany's passion for flying. Jones's prescient observations about the importance of air supremacy had first surfaced in an article he wrote about civil aviation in the Soviet Union for the December issue of *Air* magazine after his 1930 visit to the Soviet Union. Additionally, he had witnessed theatrical performances routinely interrupted with gas-mask drills in the name of Soviet Civil Defense. And Germany was no different as gas-mask demonstrations were given "in the most remote parts of the country." Goering's plan was to "blacken the European sky with a host of German squadrons."[19]

Jones confessed to being startled by the display, particularly by the men and women marching through the aerodrome grounds "in that grey-blue uniform which is becoming as much the darling of the Prussian crowd as was the most resplendent of Guards' uniforms in 1914." The implication was clearly ominous but the delivery lightened with a pun on being fashionably attired to do war. Jones admitted to a fascination with the spectacular nature of Nazi iconography. Lochner was another journalist who recognized that uniforms had been instituted as an integral part of Nazi identity, a deliberate repudiation of the republic's laws against it. Jones ended the piece with a final reminder – Germany Must Become a Nation of Aviators – one of the many propaganda messages that were being "driven into the minds of the German people by pamphlet, cinema, and radio."[20]

The fact that he failed to mention that newspapers were among the media organisations being taken over by the Nazis was arguably an oversight rather than a deliberate omission as he had made the point in several other articles. Additionally, he knew Scheffer had become editor of the *Berliner Tageblatt* in April, after the paper was shut down and its Jewish owner removed. For a time, the newspaper had fulfilled Goebbels's desire to have "a paper which was read abroad and did not make the impression that it was a propaganda sheet."[21] However, the attempt to maintain an independent newspaper in the capital of the Third Reich proved difficult despite Scheffer's intent "to create a place, from which the tyranny of madness would not, indeed, allow itself to be excluded, but where the exactly opposite, tradition conscious point of view could still find expression in new forms."[22] In due time, Goebbels reneged on his promise, of course, and no newspaper was free to publish anything other than Nazi propaganda.

In his weekly letter to family, Jones complained when Czech authorities had not responded to his request to allow him access, ruining his plans to travel beyond Prague. "That kind of thing must be a Slav characteristic." Jones also expressed ambivalence about Germany.

> My feelings about Germany are mixed. I was surprised at the freedom with which a large number of people expressed to me their antagonism to the government. The disillusionment is great. At the same time on the surface everybody looked just the same. Indeed, Germany <u>looks</u> more prosperous than Britain.... Herzog has become a storm trooper!!! ... Hitler is in rather a bad way in Germany, heaps of grumbling and a severe crisis (economic) about to break. There's great disillusion. But have practically no new material, because the English papers are far better informed than are the Germans.[23]

That Jones confessed ambivalence towards Germany should not be surprising in the light of the increasing Nazification of the country during 1933, such as the enactment of a law legitimating revocation of naturalizations and the annulment of German citizenship to people according to racial principles. This law directly targeted Jews, especially those who had emigrated from Eastern Europe.

Despite his ambivalence, Jones maintained contact with his German friends, especially the Haferkorns, who spent part of every year in Great Britain, usually with visits to Barry, and to Aberystwyth to lecture at the university. Having joined the National Socialist Party in 1933, Haferkorn earned positive comments from his superiors, described in one report as "a very reliable National Socialist, he speaks his mind openly, he takes care in good companionship and his worldly wise outlook and secure thoughtful judgement, was many times of valuable service to me."[24] Haferkorn counted on the Jones family as a solid part of that good companionship, and they were graciously welcoming. To what extent Haferkorn used that friendship to further Nazi ideology is certainly debatable.

Jones published only one article, "Fear of an Economic Storm in Germany," before returning to Wales. In the article, Jones recounted a conversation he had with a Stormtroop leader who was "typical of many hundreds of thousands of Nazis throughout the country who see that, although Germany has been immersed in a bath of the most thoroughgoing nationalism, the goal of Socialism is as distant as ever."[25]

Private ownership of businesses and property was still dominant and an anathema to these National Bolsheviks, as Jones identified them. Using a joke popular at that time, featuring one Stormtrooper asking another how he liked his troop, Jones notes the reply of "Just fine. There's only one fellow I don't like, and he's the Stormtroop leader. As matter of fact, I believe he is a Nazi!"[26] The discontent of the socialist left mirrored moderates' fear of economic collapse.

Jones reported that people in Berlin were hurriedly buying clothes and boots because, as the value of the German mark fell, prices were soaring; a situation that had been exacerbated by Germany's attempt to cut back on imports of wool and raw materials. "Everywhere the drying up of foreign currency resources was accepted as the proof that a grave economic storm was threatening and might break soon." Jones concluded the piece by outlining how Hitler was mitigating several problems, including restoring "order to public life and that he has put an end to the political murders which were a stain on German life."[27] Jones may have been right at that time, but events over the next few months proved the Nazis were still capable of murder by execution and assassination.

'a profound contempt'

Jones was in still in Germany when the purge of the SA took place on June 30, 1934, with the murder of leader Ernst Röehm, who up to that time held sway over 3.5 million Brownshirts. In "Behind the Drama of Germany," Jones explained what had happened to Roehm and his followers. Hitler himself presided over the arrest and execution. General Schleicher and his family were also executed; the supposed socialist tendencies of this wing of the Brownshirts doomed them.

In the article, although Jones focused on the plot's ingredients, in the lede he decried Hitler's "ruthless revenge against the plotters. The plotters are dead. Roehm's place has been taken by a man with whom I lunched a year ago in the train between Berlin and Hanover – Victor Lutze. I have rarely met a man who impressed me so much by his ruthlessness, grimness, lack of humour and fanaticism."[28] Jones managed to work in anecdotal information based on that earlier conversation, leading him to suppose that Lutze, having "a profound contempt for anything intellectual ... which was obvious from the unacademic tone of his language and the naïveté of his ideas,"[29] would undoubtedly help Hitler crush the opposition. Further specifics of the revenge killings were noted in Jones's diary, recording a conversation with Hans Otto Meissner, Jr.

> M[eissner] was present at the shooting that night of 19 [SA men] and saw [Max] Ernst shot. [M said,] 'My friend was the man who gave the command.'
>
> 'Were they really guilty? I asked.
>
> 'Definitely, he said. 'He's the man who [would] not hurt a fly.'
>
> 'The prisoners were not told of their sentence.... Ernst did not die well. He did not know he was going to be shot when he came out of the court. I was there. He looked up and saw the S.S. men with

Alexander Wienerberger's photograph of a sign that reads, "The burial of corpses is strictly forbidden here!" Part of a collection he donated to Cardinal Theodor Innitzer.

rifles. He was dragged before the lights of motorcars. He shouted. 'You can't shoot me. You can't shoot me.' One S.A. man said for himself, 'I'll give my command.' He said, 'Shoot.'[30]

Jones also recorded Meissner in early June saying that Hitler had been too loyal to people like Schleicher. "Foreign policy is a catastrophe. Austria won't become Nazi for a long time. Most people would support the Govt because of a lack of alternative.... We've only begun with the Jews. There will be a new campaign."[31] This foreboding message Jones failed to include in any newspaper article, even as he grew increasingly wary of Nazi intolerance.

'disastrous outlook'

When Jones returned from his trip to Germany, he delivered an address to the Cardiff Rotary Club in which he discussed how the

130

economic crisis had lessened public confidence in Hitler. Jones predicted that Goering, and Himmler's SS Blackshirts, would grow in importance: "Hitler will probably move towards the right and the dictatorship will become more severe."[32] Jones also explained that conditions were grave, and a crisis loomed. "I was impressed by the disastrous outlook of the harvest. This forebodes evil for next winter, for Germany has little foreign currency to import foodstuffs."[33] Despite this grim forecast, Jones separated the ruthless methods of Nazi leadership from the German masses, telling his audience that travelers could rest assured that they would be treated hospitably and would be as secure there as in any country.

In late June, Jones interviewed William Randolph Hearst, the American newspaper publisher who owned St. Donat's Castle, at Llantwit Major. The topics covered in the Q & A format included war debts and reparations, the League of Nations, Welsh characteristics, American naval power, and FDR's response to the Depression. Jones described Hearst's belief that a lasting, universal peace might be possible again – as it had been in the "Peace of Rome" – and "that a cooperative union of English-speaking peoples could accomplish the same beneficial results."[34] Those results were only possible if Great Britain and the United States worked together to make sure that the peace and security of the world be maintained. Jones described for Hearst his flight with Hitler, which may have, in part, hastened Hearst's desire to meet Hitler, an event which took place in August. Jones also challenged Hearst to clarify remarks about "Welshing on debts," now that he was living in Wales, and his description of Hearst's reply is candid.

> Mr. Hearst has definitely a sense of humour. He twinkled in the first part of his reply and then grew serious. "'Welshing on a debt' is a phrase devised by Englishmen to gratify the vanities and prejudices of Englishmen," he said.[35]

For his part, Jones took advantage of opportunities the interview at St. Donat's presented him – Hearst newspapers had published Jones's famine stories in 1933 and would publish three more in early 1935; another American newspaper man visiting Hearst at the time offered to hire Jones for consulting. "Paul Block offers me £100 and expenses if I accompany him over Europe for a fortnight. I don't think it is possible – it's Eisteddfod time."[36] Despite having a reason not to go, Jones eventually decided to accept Block's offer, a decision that within a few weeks would become one he regretted as the two men didn't get on, as evidenced in Jones's correspondence.

By July 26, Jones traveled to Paris via Dunkirk, staying at the Hotel Continental where he prepared several memoranda for Block. Almost all letters on this journey were written on hotel stationery, and during his time with Block, frustration and exasperation became recurring themes. Uncertainty and a lack of shared values only made matters worse. "I do not know whether Mr. Block and I are going to Berlin at 7:15 this evening or not.... I am so very sorry but I shall not be at the Eisteddfod. Mr. Block is very anxious that I should stay with him and go to a number of capitals.... We may go tomorrow or Thursday to Prague and then on to Vienna! It's fantastic how these Americans rush about.... Tonight we leave for Vienna at 11 o'clock and where we go afterwards I have no idea... I'd give anything to come back for the Eisteddfod."[37]

Jones prepared a report for Block on France, which he reworked into an article mailed to the *Western Mail*, and published on August 3, "France Does Not Expect War at Present," in which Jones characterized French glee over Hitler's inept foreign policy. "They feel malicious pleasure in the discomfiture of the little man with the Austrian accent, whose one dream – to unite his humorous, lackadaisical, and lovable fellow-countrymen with the more disciplined millions of the German Reich – has by the failure of the Vienna coup been converted into a nightmare of the most terrifying order."[38] The French, Jones wrote, were calm, believing Hitler's desire to unite Germany with Austria faced too many impediments. Those were tenuous compensations, Jones concluded, based on France's belief that Italy would be forced to seek its friendship.

Jones cabled his editor at the *Western Mail*, Mr. J. A. Sandbrook, who instructed Jones to stay with Block for as long as he was needed because the memoranda Jones prepared for Block also served as source material for his newspaper articles. Working was rushed, prompting Jones to complain: "Have any of my articles appeared? They are rather bad, because they have had to be written at queer hours and in sleeping coaches. So it has been a terrific rush.... When

I shall be home I do not know. Mr. Sandbrook did not say in his cable how long I should remain in Europe."[39]

By the time they arrived in Vienna on August 5, Jones had lost all patience with his American employer and rejoiced when, finally, they parted ways. "He says he may want me to work for him when he goes to Rome in about a week or two, but I do not think I shall go. He is terrible, vulgar, cheap, objectionable, with no respect for tradition or feeling." The rancor Jones developed in a brief time became palpable, as he was increasingly exasperated with Block's lack of discretion, juvenile quips, and rude comments. Nonetheless, Jones certainly appreciated the fiscal reward. On the final pages of one notebook, Jones recorded numerous quotes of Block, all of them betraying the American's lack of culture, education, and refinement.

'in clover'

At this point, Jones focused his attention on the Nazi murder of Engelbert Dollfuss, producing an eight-part series on the German-Austria crisis that ran from August 8-23 in the *Western Mail*. Similar to the newspaper adverts of his previous journeys to Germany, the newspaper alerted readers that Jones "will visit various capitals of Europe and his articles to the *Western Mail & South Wales News* will give the results of first-hand information and observation of the present disturbances and political movements."[40] Despite having already filed two stories on the latest crisis, Jones was described as "a special *Western Mail and South Wales News* correspondent, from Berlin."[41] Jones had already portrayed Dollfuss as the Biblical David standing up to a Hitleresque Goliath, although Jones ended that story with a German journalist whispering ominously in his ear.

In a letter to family, Jones explained his plans, which were far from set. "Tomorrow evening I intend going somewhere in South Austria and walking. I may go into Italy. I am sorry I can give no address. At the end of the week or beginning of next week I shall probably go to Berlin in order to be there for the election of August 19. Mr. Sandbrook wired me to remain in Europe but did not say how long. But I expect I shall be in Germany for the Aug. 19 election."[42]

Before departing Vienna, Jones basked in the accolades he heard from several journalists. "I got into touch at once with journalists here. I discover to my amazement that here in Vienna I am famous!! because of my Russian articles and also because the Cardinal referred to me. So I am in clover and am meeting most interesting people."[43] Having experienced both adulation and criticism, Jones relished the attention heaped on him in Vienna. To be associated with the Cardinal's calls for international relief brought Jones a measure of celebrity he could not avoid, not that he would want to shy away from it. Having declared himself an avowed pacifist and liberal, having visited several camps supported by the Society of Friends, having used personal letters sent to the German Evangelicals, Jones consistently associated himself with non-governmental organizations commissioned to relieve suffering.

'steel helmets'

Not surprisingly, Jones used the threat of famine to frame his first article, "The Forces That Are Menacing Hitler." Jones made the case that Hitler's first enemy was hunger, as the grain harvest was down, the potato fields had yielded little, and prices were soaring so that rationing cards had to be introduced. The second force against Hitler was spiritual. "The intellectuals are ashamed of the excesses of the Nazi regime and of the shame of Germany before the world. But, alas! the German cultured citizens have not the courage and the independence of their counterparts in Britain and their voices will not carry far."[44] This indictment against German intellectuals for not having sufficient courage to challenge Nazi excesses was tempered with the understanding that those challenges were ultimately doomed to fail because Nazi propaganda drowned out all internal criticism.

Jones then catalogued the catastrophic effects of Hitler's foreign policy – the hatred of Italy, the murder of Dollfuss, the strengthening of Soviet Russia's diplomatic position, and the alienation of the sympathies of all civilised peoples because of the barbarities of National Socialism against the Jews. These constituted an outline for the articles to come, the most dramatic of which Jones set in the wake of the assassination of Dollfuss in Vienna's streets.[45]

> Three soldiers in steel helmets standing near a machine gun, a lorry full of police with rifles rushing past; armed men on every corner, and a grim grey building from whose windows a few prisoners looked out – such was the scene that confronted me this morning when I penetrated the forbidden zone of Vienna.[46]

Putting himself at the very center of conflict was nothing new for Jones, and that flirtation with danger eventually resulted in his murder at the hands of Chinese bandits in Manchukuo the following August. Jones explained his British passport had enabled him to stroll through Vienna's desolate streets.

The assassination of Dollfuss had brought to the fore all of the dissension lingering directly beneath the surface. While the Austrian troops gave a superficial impression of strength and loyalty, antipathy for the regime's brutal imprisonment of thousands of workers seethed. Jones noted, "The Nazis are strong throughout the country, although the savagery of the murder of Dollfuss and the failure of the secret Stormtroopers to rise through the country have caused a set-back, but, I believe, a temporary set-back."[47]

Jones proved correct in his assumption that the Austrian administration had withstood the Nazi coup largely because of fears that Italian troops would occupy Austria if the Nazis came to power. He ended the article by pointing to Carinthia as "the first battlefield of a European war, if another breaks out"[48] because of its strategic geography where Italy, Austria, and Yugoslavia formed borders.

Jones used two pocket notebook diaries to record interviews and observations as he traveled from Vienna to Trieste with stops in Graz, Bleiberg, Klagenfurt – from where he posted two stories – continuing on to Villach, Tarvis, Udine, and Montfalcone. The notebooks bear testament to Jones's conversations with many people he encountered on this journey.

In every story, Jones was an active participant via his interactions with the people he sought out, including young people, officials, a toymaker, and an innkeeper. Using their occupation rather than name provided a shortcut to character and ready-made discourse. Participatory journalists create scaffolding for what they want to write by experiencing directly the material world around them, and recording sensory details and impressions. Traveling the equivalent of third class was a deliberate and strategic way of encountering pedestrian, nameless people, who told their particular story by answering his direct questions.

Jones probed people's sentiments and reactions to current events. The technique allowed him to work quickly and directly from his notes. The correspondence between the 1934 pocket notebook transcriptions and the published newspaper articles is easy to follow, similar to the 1933 journey to the Soviet Union.

Jones wrote four stories that the *Western Mail* published over four consecutive days from August 14-17, and the probable lag from composition to publication was approximately five days as Jones wrote on August 13, from the Hotel Wagner in Vienna, that he was that evening attending a Goering speech, the report of which was published on August 18. That would place Jones in the southern Austrian countryside towards Trieste between August 9-14. The four stories included "'Sacred Crusade' to Unite Austria with Germany," "Where War May Come From," "Italy's Big Guns Point Towards Austria," and "Vatican versus Mussolini." He spent more than a day in Trieste, managing to interview the Bishop of Trieste before heading to Berlin. Once Jones arrived in Berlin for the elections, he posted three additional articles to complete the 1934 series dealing with Hitler's Nazi Germany.

'nut in the nutcracker' (II)

The four stories from this train trip constitute an exemplar of Jones's journalistic, linguistic, and rhetorical skill-set. Fluent in French, German, and Russian, he could start up conversations with anyone, anywhere, and that overcame most difficulties inherent in traveling through Europe. He situated these articles in the border towns between Austria, Yugoslavia, and Italy, where, locals told him, armies would march if Austria went over to Hitler. A Yugoslav customs official used a map to show Jones how Italy would travel the pass at Tarvis, punctuated with local color: "... and we shall be like a nut in the nutcracker of our enemy, Italy."[49] This phrase, unlike other conversations, does not appear in the notebook diary though Jones would have remembered something so evocative, having used it to describe Danzig's position within the Polish Corridor. Perhaps Jones was creating his own verisimilitude.

Jones contextualized the larger political and economic questions as a way to give relevance to the people he encountered. He created immediacy and scope by beginning with the encouragement of "a Viennese politician ... to head south and walk in the districts where there was bloodshed..."[50] Departure at night from a train station created suspense and anticipation. Jones reported having spent a sleepless night "on hard third-class benches" heading into the mountains of south Austria where 500 Nazi troops had only recently marched into the town of Saint Veit, "hoisted the swastika flag, and tore down from the church the banners of mourning for Dollfuss"[51] until they we were bombarded by artillery and forced to escape.

As he trekked through the countryside outside Klagenfurt, he encountered a farmer who described how the Nazis had terrorized the villagers during the attack, "but now the prisons are full of them. Why, there's one village I know just near where there are only three men left. All the others have been taken or have fled across the border into Yugoslavia."[52] As Jones continued walking, he saw notices of the "Declaration of Martial Law: From July 26 all houses must be closed at eight o'clock." However, what surprised him the most was the attitude of people with whom he spoke, especially the mayor and the old headmaster of the village school. "When I heard the remark, 'The Nazis who rose here were not rebels or terrorists. It was a noble rising of the people,' I was bewildered."[53] They told Jones that 99% of the young people were Nazis. When Jones asked to speak with some young people, the mayor laughed ironically. "They're all in prison because they are Nazis.... There will be more revolts, more fighting, more bloodshed, for Austria will not have rest until we have joined with our German brothers to the north."[54]

Jones attributed support by these people for *Anschluss* with Germany to prolonged depressed prices for their agricultural products and for timber. "Propaganda has been smuggled in across the frontiers and the peasants are ready to believe all the stories of happiness and wealth which they read of in Germany."[55]

As Jones enjoyed a meal of Wiener Schnitzel and coffee, he was approached by a young man who had been sent by the mayor. "His serious blue eyes revealed the earnestness, the intolerance, and the courage of the fanatic. But Europe today is full of such fanatics."[56] When Jones asked whether or not the Roman Catholic Church would keep the government in power, the young man replied that he, like so many other Catholics, hated the way the Vatican was carrying out Mussolini's policies. "The Vatican is Italian in spirit and Italian in its foreign aims."[57] Jones concluded the article by posing another question, whether or not Italy would march into the region were Austria and Germany to unite. "That question I shall seek to answer in my next article." Jones was working quickly and provided himself with a convenient way to end one article and set up the next.

'troops, troops, troops'

Written while *en route* and datelined Trieste, the next two stories describe crossing into Italy and heading towards the Adriatic Sea. The first article, set in Trieste's center, is organized around three impressions: troops, hatred, and fear. As he crossed the border into Italy, Jones wrote in his notebook:

> Italian frontier. Six big guns. Hundreds of tents. Camouflaged also under trees. Troops in grey-green uniforms. Numbers of horses. Fires burning. Fortress looks over valley. New road being built. Dripping wet. Waterfalls.[58]

His notes became a description in the published article:

> My first impression is troops, troops, troops. As soon as the train had crossed the pass from Austria and had arrived at the frontier station of Tarvis (a name which may well be more important in the future, for Tarvis and the Brenner Pass as the two main entries from Italy into Austria) I saw in the pine forests for miles along the railway track

hundreds upon hundreds of camouflaged tents of curious square shape like bathing tents painted, grey, green a dirty orange, and a smudged red. The smoke of many camp fires hovered over the woods and Italian soldiers looked up at the passing express and waved.[59]

Jones's second impression was extracted from an Italian Fascist who boarded the train in Udine. In the notebook, Jones wrote: "A dark, excitable Fascist (badge) entered compartment. We spoke French. The Germans are savages. Hitler is a barbarian. Mussolini will never forgive him because he has broken all his promises. The moment Austria becomes Nazi & joins with Germany, we'll march over the border. The troops are ready, 40,000 of them in Tarvis. The Brenner district are full of them.... Germany we'll never forgive, never trust. Their methods are too brutal."[60]

Jones added several specific traits to flesh out his character. "What gestures of passion! How vehemently his eyes flashed at the very mention of Germany! Like a Machine-gun spitting out fire..."[61] How to flesh out individuals without resorting to caricature requires deftness, the danger being a one-dimensional voice who personifies a slogan. Deliberate typecasting was a necessary part of Jones's desire to focus on the conflict between combatants and mortal enemies whose positions had already hardened.

The third impression was the fear that if Austria joined with Germany, Hitler would set his sights on Trieste. Noting that the city had four Italian shipping lines that sailed around Africa, Jones speculated that Mussolini would not allow Austria to join with Germany "without a grim struggle."[62]

In the final story, Jones also predicted a different type of war – between the Catholic Church and Mussolini's Fascist State – would soon break out: "I have good authority for stating ..."[63] The article mentioned the Bishop of Trieste as a source of information for a topic Jones had written about throughout his career, the religious rights of a minority people living within a foreign nation. "The region around Trieste, which borders on Yugoslavia, is to Italy what Wales is to Britain."[64]

In this case, the Italians attempted to crush the Slovene language in a region around Trieste where more than a million Slovenes spoke their Slavic language. The Italians had forbidden Slovenes from publishing a prayer book in the Slovene language, priests had been imprisoned, and agreements had been broken. Jones explained that priests accused the Fascists of breaking the Concordat, which Hitler had signed in August 1933 with Pope Pius XI. The conversation Jones recorded in the notebook covered these ideas, and provided additional perspective. While previously Jones used Welsh to protect the identity of his sources, here he used it for emphasis.

Dyn mwyaf yr Eglwys [the most senior man in the Church]
    Fascists breaking Concordat.
    Mussolini is not so strong.
    Number of leaders imprisoned. A big struggle between Church & State coming. Weakness of Pope.
    But Pope is right not to maintain the Austrian govt. If Austria goes Nazi, the Austrian Catholics will be treated like the German Catholics. Terrible. Hitler cannot be trusted. His word is worth nothing. Here the fight Church v. State is double: a) language b) soul of the child.
    But the population is for me. They imprisoned people who shouted, "Up with the Bishop!"
    A false communique was sent out signed by 9 members of _____ but 8 were for me.
    There is a terrific amount of swindle in Fascism.
    In one village the head of Fascists showed a telegram which he said came from Mussolini; that he is against me. It was falsified.
    Mussolini is not told of what is happening. He is told by local starace that everyone is against me. I should probably have to go.
    The Vatican is afraid to tell Mussolini. But 3 important bishops represent one-fifth of Italy met to send a protest to Mussolini because the Fascists are taking the children away from the Church. The protest went on to the Vatican, but there they said it was not the time to disturb Mussolini.
    There are too many authorities here; the local and the Fascist secretary, and as one knows which is master.
    Here the starace is a tyrant sends false news about me.
    The Pope doesn't stand up for me enough.
    Why should a child who speaks Slovene have to learn their prayers in Italian?

It is antagonizing them from the Church.

A struggle will come. There will have to be a new agreement with Mussolini.

He thinks too much, "L'État, ç'est moi."

There is also the principle of Church & State.

They've arrested a large number of party leaders; fear that there is dissension within the camp.

They imprisoned the priests.

What's the use of Mussolini standing up for the Catholics in Austria & Germany if he attacks them in his own country?

[At top of page] The boy with luggage said, "Mussolini won't come here. He is afraid.[65]

Falsified documents, imprisoned supporters of the Bishop, the lack of papal support, all of these complaints Jones chose not to use in the published article, even though the Bishop confessed that in all likelihood, he would have to go. The specter of Mussolini as tyrant looms large in these notes, while the Pope failed to "stand up for me enough." These notes provide evidence of what constituted "his good authority" to write about the two themes of Jones's published article. Jones made the information pertinent for Welsh readers. "Imagine the revolt which would spread through Wales if Welsh Prayer Books were abolished!"[66]

'the same note of hysteria'

Having completed and mailed his fourth article in as many days, Jones found a moment to write his family a quick note. "Tonight, I am going to hear Goering speak. I have a press ticket. So I'll have a good view. I am wondering whether my article written near Liege reached Cardiff."[67] When Jones was traveling, he often asked his family to send clippings, often with specific instructions. "I always like to see them as soon as possible; because I do not know what I have written. Please also state whether leader page or which. They are absolutely essential in helping me to write the next ones. I sent a few more off yesterday."[68] This concern stemmed from having to write a series of articles that needed both an explainer/nut graph tying one story to the series for continuity and a news peg to generate additional interest.

With the article, "The Hysteria of Goering," Jones reported on Goering's pre-election campaign speech on August 13 in Munich. Jones captured the Nazi hysteria in the details of the spectacle – the colors, the banners, the Brownshirts, an electric swastika sign, a sign hung between colossal pillars of a temple, "With Adolph Hitler for Germany." In the middle of this panorama loomed Goering "a fat man in a brown uniform standing up and giving the Fascist salute.

Goering had arrived to speak in the "campaign for Hitler's election on Sunday."[69] Jones framed the spectacle in his description of the moments prior to Goering's arrival as quiet darkness. "Then, with a suddenness which made one's eyes blink, searchlights flashed, a military band blared out a Nazi march and hundreds upon hundreds of banners were seen approaching from the distance down the avenue towards the temple."[70]

Jones cast Goering as the high priest of National Socialism ideology, a "tragic actor" who could not help but reveal his true nature, despite the light that shined down on him. His voice boomed out with "a touch of rich harmony about it, but soon I felt a note of hardness."[71] Jones positioned himself into the story to filter the message from the trappings of the speaker's delivery. Goering's hardness, Jones noted, barked out like the clipped tones of a German officer, "a jarring sound of cruelty, impatience, and intolerance, which contrasted with the studied harmony and pleasing volume of the opening sentences."[72]

Jones explained that within the high points of his speech, Goering hit "the same note of hysteria and unbridled passion which I had heard in Hitler's speeches, a note which inspires one with fear that the speaker will suddenly break down or lose absolute control of his mental powers."[73] Despite these "purple patches" full of passion, the speaker failed to generate a transcendent moment worthy of the surroundings. "Where was the enthusiasm that filled the assembly 18 months ago? Where was the spirit of religious fervour...And those dark shadows in the trees yonder. Were they, perhaps, the ghosts of vanished Storm Troop leaders ... whose ashes are now in some nearby graveyard."[74]

In this dramatic conjuring, Jones offered his most devastating condemnation of the Nazi murders of Röehm, Schleicher, and others. Goering had presided over that hastily arranged inquest and pronounced summary judgment against SA members, yet his stature had been diminished. So ghastly had the murders been that ordinary Germans could only cringe. "Indifference is the keynote of the weak. Families are forced to listen to the speeches which are pouring through the wireless like an unceasing flood. In many houses the caretaker visits each flat to inquire who listened in and who was out, and whether the person, who was out, listened in or not."[75] Jones pointed out that true oratory cannot be force fed, and again he referenced Lloyd George, whose voice and gestures served as a model for Welsh members of Parliament. The Nazi barrage of unceasing propaganda lost meaning when people were forced to listen or lose their freedom.

Jones brought the story full circle by returning to the embodiment of Nazi brutishness, Goering's fleshy fist, "ever moving, ever threatening ... a brutal, a nailed fist."[76] Jones wrote that many days in the future, he'd be thinking not about a rigged election but about "that iron fist of Goering which I saw clenched and threatening as the lights shone down upon it in temple at Munich."[77] Memorable for all the wrong reasons, Goering's fist served as a jarring reminder that Nazi brutality was manifested in its rhetorical messaging.

Significantly, Jones admitted in the article his own "careless raptures" of the early Hitler spectacles, but he also left no doubt about his current attitude toward the Nazis. As Goering entered the temple, Jones made his statement. "The crowd stood with outstretched arms – I must have been the only one in that vast multitude whose right arm remained obstinately unraised."[78]

'what are votes'

The election results, already a foregone conclusion, Jones covered in an article, headlined "Who Are the 'Yeses' and 'No' in the German

Plebiscite," by delineating who were the voters for and against Hitler. The "Yes" votes were by Germans who "believed that he had rescued them from Bolshevism and from massacre."[79] Among those, Jones identified industrialists, because Hitler had smashed the trade unions and ended strikes. Most voted out of fear that they would be outed and lose posts.

Jones affirmed that ballots were secret. "I visited a polling booth in the most Communistic area of Berlin. There was no number or mark on my voting slip by which the voter could be identified."[80] Jones did not suggest other means of voter suppression beyond the immediate polling area, but it was an obvious concern. He returned to the topic in October when he covered elections in the Saar region. The No voters "comprise men of such scattered opinions that they could hardly organize to overthrow Hitler."[81]

In addition to communists and socialists, Jones included numbers of Catholics who rejected the Nazis' claim "to the souls of the children and to the belief of young Nazis that 'we have a new religion and that religion is Germany!'"[82] Jones was on familiar ground, having found the same blind loyalty in *Komsomoltsi*, the young Communist Pioneers for whom Bolshevism was a religion. Unimpressed with the entire election, Jones characterized it as a meaningless exercise. "What are votes, after all, to men of strong will who have energy, ruthlessness, the determination to stay in power – and machine guns?"[83]

Having provided another episode in his ongoing analysis of Nazi Germany, Jones enjoyed the comforts of Berlin. "Am having a most interesting time in Berlin," he wrote to his family. "I had a fine morning with Ivy Lee. Yesterday lunched with Paul Scheffer. He wants me to write articles for the Berliner Tageblatt."[84] Jones sporadically maintained contact with Lee, who had been devastated when a Congressional committee on un-American activities released the testimony of its hearings with Lee. Even though he had been exonerated, release of the transcripts had provided ammunition to his critics, who characterized him as the protector of not only Wall Street "Robber Barons," but also the defender of Nazi fanaticism. It is possible they discussed Germany's future under Hitler, as that was the subject of Jones's next article, "Hitler's Trump Card – Fear that Germany May Fall to Pieces."

Jones explained that Germany, unlike other countries, was not really a unified nation, "a mere geographical expression" without enduring political foundations to provide any semblance of a nation. "She has never been a real nation, but a collection of States loosely knit together and loathing each other.... Such a hotch-potch of peoples could easily fall to pieces and Germany could disappear. That is the present fear of loyal Germans."[85] And without natural frontiers except the Baltic and a discordant geography, there was little keeping Germany together.

Jones called this German longing for unity Hitler's trump card, which enabled him to mold the country to his vision. "It explains his ruthlessness in stamping out differences of opinion, differences of uniforms, differences in political parties, and differences in religious beliefs."[86] Jones had no doubt that Hitler would play that card when food ran short, and then blame the rest of the world for threatening Germany. This victimization elevated the need for a savior, which only Hitler could provide with his messianic zeal, leading the chant, *"Deutschland Uber Alles"* ["Germany above all"].

Jones deftly captured this overriding concern in his final article from Berlin by describing what he had witnessed. "I watched thousands of bareheaded Germans last Sunday singing these words with passionate religious fervour, and repeating the last lines like the congregation at a Welsh chapel. Hitler stood at the window of the Chancellery saluting his worshipers who crowded the street before the Palace."[87]

'German to the core'

Jones squeezed one last article out of the trip through central Europe, returning to minority rights. On this occasion, Jones focused on German-speaking Austrians in the South Tyrol, who, under the rule of Mussolini, were denied linguistic rights, "persecuted by the police if you formed a choir."[88] Calling it a Never-Never-Land of pure satire, Jones explained the dilemma for Austrian people displaced by the Treaty of Versailles and placed under the rule of Italy. "It plays a part because the South Tyrolese are growing violently Nazi and will be a source of internal weakness for Italy should Italian troops ever decide to cross the Brenner Pass into Austria."[89] Jones wasted few words in getting to his point: "The feeling that fellow Austrians are being enslaved by the Italians will fan the flames of another Nazi rebellion in Austria."[90]

Jones's return from his trip around Europe marked a significant juncture in his career as he now set his sights on his proposed round the world tour. That he sought out editors, in addition to those he already worked with, like W. P. Crozier of the *Manchester Guardian*, Paul Scheffer of the *Berliner Tageblatt*, and others willing to publish his articles, demonstrates his determination to chart a new course for himself.

By October 1, he declared himself a free man and recounted in his diary what Hall Williams told him while driving through Cadoxton, outside Barry. "He points out the Old Travellers Arms, now a white-washed cottage where once travellers used to call. Told me a story of how an old man went out of the cottage one day, and was never seen again. It was noticed that the grass grew greener in one spot in the garden. On digging this area up a skeleton was found."[91]

In the days prior to departing for the United States and the Far East, Jones filed two stories for the *Western Mail* about conditions in the Saar region. He interviewed Max Braun, leader of the anti-Nazi Front in Saar, about the January 1935 plebiscite that would return the area to Germany. Braun was predicting a certain bloodbath unless the vote was delayed. "We are German to the core here. That is why we are against Hitler. We want to deal a blow to the Nazi system which will resound through Germany itself."[92] Braun, threatened with a bounty on his head, accused Nazi officials of forging the vote list by changing names and purging others. Jones questioned inspectors at the voting commission, but the mistakes were "purely accidental."[93]

Jones illustrated the problems in the Saar by focusing on the mines and the availability of Lorraine ore if Saar became German. Despite interdependency, the economic advantages would follow the Saar's return to Germany and "would benefit from the improving business conditions so marked in the Germany of Hitler."[94] And as the French director of the mines told him, conversations about re-purchasing the mines in 1935 would be influenced to the detriment of France's interests.

Notebook entries chronicling Otto Meissner Jr.'s story about the murder of Max Ernst, July 1934.

The final articles on Germany leave no doubt of his overt rejection of the Nazis. In point of fact, Jones was presented with an opportunity to become Berlin correspondent for the Hearst-owned *International News* at £2000 a year. Though he found it tempting, Jones decided against being stationed in Berlin and covering Germany. If Jones needed confirmation that he was making the right decision to leave Germany behind, he doubtlessly found it in a conversation he had in Berlin with Melitta and Eric Schuler and recorded in another pocket diary dated October 5.

I was told by Melitta of the terrible fate of Idris Morgan's friend Fraulein [Gerda] Sommer, a beautiful blonde girl.

She was found dead in the apartment of Brückner, Hitler's adjutant.

The criminal police telephoned the parents long after to say, "Your daughter has been found dead. Alles ist erle digt [Everything is done]."

There was no medical examination. The criminal police seemed to be afraid of Brückner, who has a lot of power.

The maid said that Fraulein Sommer had come at 2 o'clock in the morning & had said that she had been out with Brückner & was afraid to go home. She wanted to spend the night there & she could tell her parents that she had slept with friends.

Next morning, she was found dead at 10 o'clock.

The police said gas poisoning but there is only gas in the kitchen and not enough to poison.

The parents – almost demented – wrote to Brückner. He replied that he was very busy & had to go to Munich, but would write on his return. He has never written.[95]

Jones would have remembered Wilhelm Brückner, of course, from the flight with Hitler in February 1933, having described him seated to the left of Hitler, "a big fair fellow..."[96] who was the Aryan prototype with dueling scars clearly visible on his face. Hearing about Brückner's callous treatment of the Sommer family, Jones doubtlessly envisioned the look on Brückner's scarred face when confronted with the parents' raw grief. Jones would have been as disturbed as Idris Morgan, also from Barry who was working for a year at Dresdner Bank in Berlin as part of an exchange program with his employers, Barclay's Bank.[97] Jones knew how these things transpired: Brückner was a powerful man within Hitler's inner circle, having been imprisoned with Hitler in Landsberg following the failed putsch of 1923 and appointed to chief adjutant in 1930. Engaged to a close friend of Eva Braun, Brückner could not afford any appearance of impropriety and betrayal, at a time when Goering and Goebbels were compiling a list of SA men to be purged. Gerda Sommer, Jones realized, was an inconvenience that men of Brückner's ilk made disappear.

In deciding to venture independently away from Wales to the war-torn reaches of Manchukuo, Jones left behind all that had sustained him thus far. He expected to be away six months. On assignment.

Notes

1 "Changed Policy of Hitler," *Western Mail*, January 16, 1934, 9.

2 Gareth Jones, "Hatchet Is Buried for Ten Years," *Western Mail*, January 29, 1934, 7.

3 Jones, "Hatchet," 7.

4 Jones, "Hatchet," 7.

5 Gareth Jones, "Origins of the National Eistedfodd," *Western Mail*, August 3, 1934, 3.

6 Jones, "Hatchet," 7.

7 Gareth Jones, "The World's Perplexing Problems," *Western Mail*, May 9, 1934, 9.

8 Gareth Jones, "A Socialist Tells the Truth About Moscow," *Western Mail* ["Winter in Moscow," by Malcolm Muggeridge. Eyre and Spottiswoode, 7s. 6d.], March 15, 1934, 11.

9 Jones, "A Socialist Tells," 11.

10 "Britain through Russian Eyes," *Western Mail*, March 19, 1933, 7.

11 "Britain through Russian Eyes," 7.

12 "Britain through Russian Eyes," 7.

13 Gareth Jones, Letter dated May 11, 1934. Gareth Vaughan Jones Papers, National Library of Wales, Aberystwyth, File B 6/5.

14 "Resolution of the All-Union Communist Party (Bolshevik) Politburo," September 17, 1932. RGASPI, fond 17, list 3, file 901, sheet 6.

15 H. J. Heinz, Jr., *Experiences in Russia 1931 – A Diary* (Pittsburgh, Pa.: Alton Press, 1932), 38.

16 Jones, Letter dated May 30, 1932.

17 See Gareth Jones, "My Russian Diary I," *The Star*, October 20, 1930; Journal of Russian Travels, 1931; and for the crust of bread anecdote, see H. R. Knickerbocker, "Famine Grips Russia, Millions Dying," *New York Evening Post*, March 29, 1933, 1; and Edgar Ansel Mowrer, "Russian Famine Now as Great as Starvation of 1921, Says Secretary to Lloyd George," *Chicago Daily News*, March 29, 1933, 2. Lastly, Jones published two accounts of his own "near arrest" at a train station for speaking with peasants – "Starving Russians Seething with Discontent," *Western Mail*, April 4, 1933, 1-2; "Fate of Thrifty in USSR: Gareth Jones Tells How Communists Seized All Land and Let Peasants Starve," *Los Angeles Examiner*, January 14, 1935, 4.

18 Gareth Jones, "10,000 Planes on German Frontiers," *Western Mail*, June 29, 1934, 11.

19 Jones, "10,000 Planes," 11.

20 Jones, "10,000 Planes," 11.

21 Henry Regnery, *Perfect Sowing: Reflections of a Bookman* (Wilmington, Del.: ISI Books, 1999), 237.

22 Margaret Boveri, *Wür lügen alle* (Berlin: Olten and Freiburg, 1965), 135.

23 Gareth Jones, Letter dated June 10, 1934. Gareth Vaughan Jones Papers, National Library of Wales, Aberystwyth, File B6/5.

24 Biography of Reinhard Haferkorn, accessed from http://discovery.nationalarchives.gov.uk/SearchUI/details?Uri=C11050176.

25 Gareth Jones, "Fear of an Economic Storm in Germany," *Western Mail*, June 25, 1934, 7.

26 Jones, "Fear," 7.

27 Jones, "Fear," 7.

28 Gareth Jones, "Behind the Drama of Germany," *Western Mail*, July 2, 1934, 8.

29 Jones, "Behind the Drama," 8.

30 Gareth Jones, Trieste Diary [Notebook], August 1934, Gareth Vaughan Jones Papers, National Library of Wales, Aberystwyth, File 41. In addition to the Meissner, Jr., interview, this notebook contains Jones's impressions at the Goering speech in Munich, and an interview with a journalist in Trieste who warns Jones not to identify him in a story as that would result with his being shot.

31 Gareth Jones, Travels in Germany, [June] 1934, Gareth Vaughan Jones Papers, National Library of Wales, Aberystwyth, File B3/17.

32 "Nazis Ruthless," *Western Mail*, July 10, 1934, 10.

33 "Nazis Ruthless," 10.

34 Gareth Jones, "World Peace in Hands of Anglo-Saxons," *Western Mail*, June 27, 1934, 9.

35 Jones, "World Peace," 9. The origin of the term "Welshing", or "Welching", meaning to renege on a debt, is unknown but it first appeared in print in the *Racing Times* in 1860 when referring to a gambler denying that he'd failed to pay his losses. George IV, as Prince Regent (and therefore Prince of Wales) had an extravagant lifestyle dominated by gambling and whose large debts were eventually paid-off by Parliament. It is possible that the Prince of Wales's unreliability when paying his gambling debts became a commonly used term for anyone reneging on a debt or deal. The term is considered highly offensive by Welsh people who were subsequently, and unjustifiably, saddled with the reputation of being untrustworthy.

36 Gareth Jones, Letter dated July 16, 1934. Gareth Vaughan Jones Papers, National Library of Wales, Aberystwyth, File B6/5.

37 Gareth Jones, Letters dated July 26, 29, 31, August 1, 1934. Gareth Vaughan Jones Papers, National Library of Wales, Aberystwyth, File B6/5.

38 Gareth Jones, "France Does Not Expect War at Present," *Western Mail*, August 3, 1934, 11.

39 Gareth Jones, Letter dated August 3, 1934. Gareth Vaughan Jones Papers, National Library of Wales, Aberystwyth, File B6/5.

40 "Mr Gareth Jones," *Western Mail*, August 2, 1934, 9.

41 Gareth Jones, "The Forces That Are Menacing Hitler," *Western Mail*, August 8, 1934, 9.

42 Gareth Jones, Letter dated August 5, 1934. Gareth Vaughan Jones Papers, National Library of Wales, Aberystwyth, File B6/5.

43 Jones, Letter dated August 5.

44 Jones, "The Forces Menacing," 9.

45 Gareth Jones, "Three Catastrophes in a Month," *Western Mail*, August 2, 1934, 9.

46 Gareth Jones, "Austria Torn by Dissension and Flaming with Hatred," *Western Mail* August 10, 1934, 8.

47 Jones, "Austria Torn," 8.

48 Jones, "Austria Torn," 8.

49 Gareth Jones, "Where War May Come From," *Western Mail*, August 15, 1934, 9.

50 Gareth Jones, "'Sacred Crusade' to Unite Austria with Germany," *Western Mail*, August 14, 1934, 11.

51 Jones, "Sacred Crusade," 11.

52 Jones, "Sacred Crusade," 11.

53 Jones, "Sacred Crusade," 11.9.

54 Jones, "Sacred Crusade," 11.

55 Jones, "Sacred Crusade," 11.

56 Jones, "Sacred Crusade," 11.

57 Jones, "Sacred Crusade," 11.

58 Gareth Jones, Tour of Central Europe 1934. Gareth Vaughan Jones Pagers, National Library of Wales, Aberystwyth, File B3/15.

59 Gareth Jones, "Italy's Big Guns Point towards Austria," *Western Mail*, August 16, 1934, 9.

60 Jones, Tour of Central Europe 1934.

61 Jones, "Italy's Big Guns," 9.

62 Jones, "Italy's Big Guns," 9.

63 Gareth Jones, "Vatican versus Mussolini," *Western Mail*, August 17, 1934, 9.

64 Jones, "Vatican," 9.

65 Jones, Tour of Central Europe 1934.

66 Jones, "Vatican," 9.

67 Gareth Jones, Letter dated August 13, 1934, Gareth Vaughan Jones Papers, National Library of Wales, Aberystwyth, File B6/5.

68 Gareth Jones, Letter dated February 12, 1933, Gareth Vaughan Jones Papers, National Library of Wales, Aberystwyth, File B6/4.

69 Gareth Jones, "The Hysteria of Goering," *Western Mail*, August 18, 1934, 9.

70 Jones, "Hysteria," 9.

71 Jones, "Hysteria," 9.

72 Jones, "Hysteria," 9.

73 Jones, "Hysteria," 9.

74 Jones, "Hysteria," 9.

75 Jones, "Hysteria," 9.

76 Jones, "Hysteria," 9.

77 Jones, "Hysteria," 9.

78 Jones, "Hysteria," 9.

79 Gareth Jones, "Who Are the 'Yeses' and 'Noes' in the German Plebiscite," *Western Mail*, August 21, 1934, 11.

80 Jones, "Who Are," 11.

81 Jones, "Who Are," 11.

82 Jones, "Who Are," 11.

83 Jones, "Who Are," 11.

84 Gareth Jones, Letter dated August 19, 1934, Gareth Vaughan Jones Papers, National Library of Wales, Aberystwyth, File B6/5.

85 Gareth Jones, "Hitler's Trump Card – Fear That Germany May Fall to Pieces," *Western Mail*, August 22, 1934, 9.

86 Jones, "Hitler's Trump Card," 9.

87 Jones, "Hitler's Trump Card," 9.

88 Gareth Jones, "Austrians 'Enslaved' by Italy," *Western Mail*, August 23, 1934, 9.

89 Jones, "Austrians Enslaved," 9.

90 Jones, "Austrians Enslaved," 9.

91 Gareth Jones, Travels in the United States, Gareth Vaughan Jones Papers, National Library of Wales, Aberystwyth, File B3/16.

92 Gareth Jones, "A St. Bartholomew's Night on the Saar," *Western Mail*, October 25, 1934, 9.

93 Jones, "St. Bartholomew's Night," 9.

94 Gareth Jones, "Will France Withhold Lorraine Iron Ore from the Saar?" *Western Mail*, October 26, 1934, 8.

95 Gareth Jones, Diary of a Trip to Germany, 1934, Gareth Vaughan Jones Papers, National Library of Wales, Aberystwyth, File 42.

96 Gareth Jones, Hitler Diary, 1933. Gareth Vaughan Jones Papers, National Library of Wales, Aberystwyth, File B1/9.

97 Geraint Talfan Davies, The Girl in the Diary, BBC One, Wales. 12 August 2014. Accessed English transcript from https://subsaga.com/bbc/entertainment/gohebwyr/cyfres-1/geraint-talfan-davies.html.

7
Denial, Distortion, and Intellectual Pathology

Denial

This study has unpacked the major tropes that journalist Gareth Jones used to report on Hitler's dictatorship in Nazi Germany, utilizing critical discourse analysis to delineate the topics and journalistic techniques employed as well as the political, cultural, religious, and economic contexts within which he worked. These articles by Jones constitute important discursive threads delineating issues confronting Germany in the first half of the 1930s. Recent work by journalism historians to show how reporters covered that emerging German dictatorship has contributed to our understanding of the Third Reich's Final Solution.

While Jones was certainly not the first or only journalist to write about Hitler and the Nazis, his articles warrant consideration given his unique position of having reported mass starvation in Ukraine at the time Hitler became chancellor. Jones's reporting on the Soviet Union provided material propaganda to the Nazis, as did the other reporters who covered the famine in Ukraine SSR.

As Jones was fond of saying, it does not take "a particularly nimble mind" to imagine that every time a reporter criticized a Communist Party member, it could be distorted to mean he was criticizing a Jew-Bolshevik. And every time a reporter mentioned how much the peasants hated the communists, it showed hatred of Jews. If that rhetorical parameter is the applicable standard, then any mention of one impugns the other and becomes antisemitic. For example, in his report to the Wheat Board, Andrew Cairns suggested Soviet agriculture would be better off without Jews. Cairns could only hope "... that they [Fourth International] had reluctantly found it necessary to fire all the Jews and other town birds managing white elephants called State grain and cattle factories, communes and many of the collectives, as despite their admirable qualifications to accept and expound the teachings of Marx and Lenin, unfortunately they knew little or nothing about farming..."[1]

The canard that Jews ruined Soviet agriculture, oversaw dekulakization, and organized the blacklisting of villages became fodder for nationalists eager for retribution. Holocaust researchers have argued that blaming the Jews because they had participated in Bolshevik actions became one of many motives rationalizing Ukrainian collaboration with the Nazis beginning in the summer of 1941, after the Soviets evacuated western Ukraine.[2] Such a reading fosters interpretations of Gareth Jones as a Nazi antisemite; the transformation of code words enables a competing narrative that serves a very specific purpose of calling into question Jones's motives. It's a short journey from there to complete dismissal of his reporting of mass starvation in Ukraine as Nazi propaganda, a lie perpetrated against the Soviet Union, a journalistic hoax, and a precursor of today's fake news.

Authoritarianism abides only its own alternative facts; all else deceives. That Nazis were prosecuted and found guilty as war criminals at Nuremburg while no Bolsheviks were ever brought up on charges of crimes against humanity, let alone admit responsibility or offer reparations to Ukraine as a sovereign nation, remains a case of justice denied for Ukrainians and defenders of human rights.

I argue that this misrepresentation of Jones's work is an extreme form of genocide denial by way of the ontological turn to relativism: That because he was critical of the Soviet Union, he must have been supportive of the Nazis. Analysis reveals that his reporting on Hitler and the German dictatorship in both the February and June series of 1933, and the Night of the Long Knives series in August 1934, disproves that bifurcation. Jones, an avowed pacifist and liberal, criticized Nazi fanaticism in no uncertain terms, calling it "the most volcanic nationalist awakening which the world has seen" that was

155

careering "full speed ahead towards a Fascist dictatorship." Deducing that Jones wrote these words while colluding with the Nazis is an exercise in wishful thinking mired in dubious reasoning tethered to a long list of circumstantial, but misleading, details.

The denigration of Jones has always played a pivotal role in denials of the *Holodomor*. Labeling him a Nazi collaborator/sympathizer has remained a staple in the famine-genocide deniers' counter-narrative. That argument purposefully dismisses several realities: that Hitler had knowledge about Soviet agricultural conditions before Jones ventured there, that Jones was neither the first nor the only western journalist to write about mass starvation in the Soviet Union, and that Germany was the principal trade partner with the Soviet Union and continued to rely on Soviet exports, ultimately signing the Molotov-Ribbentrop Pact of non-aggression in 1939 and paving the way for an invasion of Poland from east and west.

To illustrate how Jones is attacked, consider a website review of Agnieszka Holland's 2018 film "Mr Jones" in which the reviewer for thecommunists.org relativizes factual history by inventing interesting, but empty narratives, intended "to expose and confront the fraudulent depiction of Gareth Jones"[3] and his reporting of the *Holodomor*. It typifies the twisted logic of genocide denial, replete with factual inaccuracies, insinuation, and guilt by association to cast doubt on the actual reporting. By calling into question Jones's having reported about Hitler, Goebbels, and Goering, after attending the Frankfurt rally, as well as covering other speeches, air shows, and Nazi parades, *Holodomor* deniers attempt to delegitimize and debunk what is accepted historical fact – as recorded in a large body of Soviet documents no less. Then the reviewer offers these alternate facts:

> Nothing, however, is said of the fact that his journey to Soviet Ukraine began and ended in Nazi Germany, where he was the guest of Adolf Hitler.... The jovial arsonists [of the Reichstag fire] Hitler and Goebbels took Mr Jones to Nazi party rallies and, after his deportation from the USSR, Mr Jones was back in Berlin on 29 March 1933 to tell the German people all about the horrors he had witnessed in the Soviet Union.... These real falsifiers of history need to be exposed and confronted for the barefaced liars that they are.[4]

The first assertion that Jones's trip began and ended in Nazi Germany is verifiably false; it is a construct of juxtaposition to insinuate something devious. In reality, his trip started and ended in Wales, not Berlin. As this study has shown, Jones completed several speaking engagements in England up until the night he left London on his way to Moscow via Berlin. Additionally, his departure from Moscow took him to Warsaw. Jones then visited Danzig, staying several days with the Haferkorns, where he composed his report to Lloyd George. Jones held his news conference in Berlin because he knew that the most influential foreign journalists were stationed there.

In a similar way, it has been insinuated that Jones was deflecting public attention away from the April 1 boycott of Jewish businesses. However, reporting about the boycott had started much earlier, and could not have been drowned out by Jones's announcement, however gruesome, as the difference in scale between the two stories was enormous. Jones was, at the time, hardly a figure who commanded that type of attention. Duranty's story denying Jones's claims appeared on page 13 of the *New York Times*; the boycott of Jewish businesses made front-page news on both March 30-31. The idea that Jones's announcement of mass starvation deflected attention away from the Nazi boycott of Jewish businesses typifies the magical thinking of famine-genocide deniers.

Accusing Jones of associating with "jovial arsonists," his flight with Hitler and Goebbels, and his singing German marches with Hanfstaengl makes it easier to disregard what he reported about that rally, not rallies, in Frankfurt. The reviewer represented Jones as reprehensible, irresponsible, immoral, and unethical. Exactly what journalistic code of ethics or good practice Jones crossed, the reviewer does not explain. Nor does s/he mention that the other journalist to accompany Hitler and Goebbels on that flight was Sefton Delmer, who was far better known than Jones and who went to considerable lengths to gain access by renting a grand piano for Hanfstaengl.[5]

Foreign journalists who came to understand the brutality of Nazi ideology did not act as a monolith, and the views found in their reporting ranged across a wide spectrum of opinion. Journalists writing at the time had no Holocaust perspective, and while several books have called journalists' failure to warn the public with greater alarm about antisemitism, the experiences of journalists attempting to raise the issue met considerable resistance from editors, politicians, and business leaders. Public indifference must be inferred from the lack of moral outrage. The same questions must be asked as to why millions of Ukrainians were starving to death at a time of the greatest surplus of wheat and few journalists broke through Soviet attempts to bury that news. Jones did. Denigrating Jones as a Nazi sympathizer is the convenient but abject means to deny the fact four million Ukrainians starved to death in 1932-1933.

Finally, the reviewer's point about Jones's deportation is factually inaccurate. Jones was never deported. Even after being escorted from a Ukrainian train station for speaking with starving peasants and deposited at the German Consulate in Khar'kiv, Jones continued his journey and interviewed Foreign Minister Litvinov and Walter Duranty, the *New York Times* correspondent, who duplicitously denigrated Jones by name in his infamous article of March 31, "Russians Hungry, But Not Starving." For his part in denigrating Jones while serving to advance U.S. recognition of Stalin's Soviet Union, Duranty has been brazenly displayed in Pulitzer Hall in the New York Times Building. Titled "For Distinguished Service to Readers," the Pulitzer Hall's introductory panel explains the importance of the prizes. "The Pulitzer Prizes are universally recognized as the most prestigious in American journalism." In Pulitzer Hall, Duranty has been prominently positioned atop the first panel with photographs and descriptions of 12 journalists. Such a display is an anathema to what journalism purports is its mission. Today's denigrators use Jones's employment with Lloyd George and reshape it into something scheming, perhaps spying because, after all, Jones was educated at Cambridge, was fluent in several languages, and seemed to have a network of contacts far beyond the reach of a journalist from Wales. Even his mother Annie's experiences in Ukraine become ingredients in a recipe for an international Jewish Consortium. Rewriting history to make it conform into a carefully wrought mold requires relentlessly making every friendship, contact, and acquaintance mean something more than what is known.

Holodomor deniers, then and now, offer nothing factual to counter the narrative found in the newspaper reporting from the time. To counter the honest reporting of Jones, Barnes, Stoneman,

Hitler addressing the Frankfurt rally. Jones, was seated with other journalists close to the stage.

Muggeridge, Schiller, Clyman, Chamberlin, Mowrer, Knickerbocker, and others, the reporting by the Hearst-financed impostor, Thomas Walker, alias Robert Green, in 1934, takes on inflated importance, held up to delegitimate every photograph and every published story about the *Holodomor*. Additionally, in the post-truth, post-survivor dystopian echo chamber, personal memoirs by Ukrainians are discounted, diasporas must be viewed as biased, and government documentation that corroborates newspaper reporting must be conveniently overlooked or deemed forgeries. What happens to history when primary source material – the letters, the memoirs, oral stories, newspaper accounts – loses meaning because the hermeneutic nature of representation is open to any interpretation?

Jones contributed three articles to Hearst newspapers in January 1935 that were little more than rehashed vitriol that emphasized Communist Party failures and state terror unleashed in retaliation for the assassination of Kirov. Jones was targeting the Communist Party leadership more than agricultural failures, since by this time Jones certainly knew that severe mass starvation had been mitigated by several harvests, and conditions he had witnessed no longer existed. That, however, should not invalidate previous reporting.

The desire to make Jones into a pre-ordained hero/villain reduces variance to hide the fact that he had defects, weaknesses, biases, and flaws. He admitted to being conceited, and he readily criticized individuals like Paul Block and public figures like George Bernard Shaw, and more broadly, called Poles second rate; American politicians were busybodies, and White Russians were unreliable. To create a portrait of Jones as only good, only righteous, and only fair is to deny his humanity.

Distortion

Because of his elevation as a "Hero of Ukraine," Jones became the most obvious person to brand as a Nazi sympathizer; in that, he was not alone. Anyone who accused the Soviet Union of hiding the famine was guilty of colluding with the Nazis to overthrow Soviet advancement. In December 1933, the *New York Times* reported that, according to Soviet authorities, a separatist movement in Ukraine was being supported by the Nazis, led by Rosenberg.[6] In exchange, Germany would receive the Polish Corridor for the east bank of the Dnieper River and an outlet through the Black Sea. Establishment of Ukraine as a bourgeois democracy was the purported goal.

The Soviets turned every threat into propaganda to show that foreign powers were planning to intervene in Soviet affairs, thereby requiring its citizens to be prepared to fight. In a letter to Kaganovich in August 1932 when grain requisitions became drastic, Stalin ordered steps to forestall a Ukrainian counter-revolution, given the "active and latent petlurites and direct agents of Pilsudski. If the situation gets any worse, these elements won't hesitate to open a front within (and outside) the Party, against the Party.... Without these and similar measures, I repeat once again: we will lose Ukraine."[7]

Only months later, Stalin ordered an end to Ukrainization, branding it a "nationalist deviation" that warranted repression of Ukrainian language and culture. What followed – taking all the grain, leaving no seed stock, blacklisting *raions* [administrative districts] that failed to meet quotas, and closing Ukraine's borders – created a humanitarian catastrophe. Recognition of the USSR by the United States in November 1933 legitimated Stalin's campaign of terror and left Ukrainians without recognition of the disaster. And so it remained until World War II changed perceptions about what constitutes genocide. As Frank Sysyn notes, Ukrainian national aspirations were contextualized within competing ideologies that tended to mute discussion of the *Holodomor*. "The importance of rightist nationalism in Ukrainian émigré political life, the collaboration of some Ukrainians with the Nazis, the history of pogroms in Ukraine and the support of the Republican Party's Captive Nations Programme by an active political leadership in the American Ukrainian community further dissuaded many scholars from examining Ukrainian topics."[8] Sysyn concludes by noting that the Soviets, having fought alongside the Allies in the war, had relative success "in making the famine issue be ignored by associating it with Nazi collaborators, particularly, for example, as they did with the Katyn massacre, when some evidence came from Nazi German sources."[9] If genocide scholarship has advanced understanding of human rights, then there should be no confusion about the difference between famine and forced mass starvation, between an act of God and state-sponsored murder.

Before Jones was foisted upon the public consciousness, media coverage of the *Holodomor* in the West was sparse. In 1986, William F. Buckley Jr. hosted a PBS airing of the documentary *Harvest of Despair*, produced by Ukrainian Famine Research Committee. Buckley, host of "A Firing Line," moderated a discussion with panelists Robert Conquest, author of *Harvest of Sorrow: Soviet Collectivization and the Terror-Famine*; Harrison Salisbury, former Moscow correspondent for the *New York Times*; and Christopher Hitchens, columnist for *The Nation*. While discussion centered around Soviet malfeasance and Duranty's complicity, Hitchens raised the issue of Ukrainian collaboration with the Nazis. As one reviewer noted, PBS and Buckley performed a public service in attempting to broaden public understanding "about a tragedy that commercial TV preferred to ignore in order to escape the inevitable controversy it will engender."[10]

That controversy was fully realized by American commercial network television more than a decade later when CBS broadcast a *60 Minutes* segment, "The Ugly Face of Freedom," on the eve of Ukrainian President Leonid Kotchma's visit to the United States. Many reviewers described the segment as distorted, factually inaccurate, and a misrepresentation of "the unsafe" conditions for Jews then living in Ukraine, given this Ukrainian ultra-nationalist fervor that CBS conjured by creating a montage that included a group of uniformed men marching and shouting *Slava Natsiye! Slava Natsiye!* [Glory to the Nation! Glory to the Nation!] followed by war footage of Jews being rounded up, then a close-up of Simon Wiesenthal being interviewed. Host Morley Safer's concluding remarks illustrate how easily racial hatred can be manipulated to malign national identity.

> The church and government of Ukraine have tried to ease people's fears, suggesting that things are not as serious as they might appear; that Ukrainians, despite the allegations, are not genetically anti-Semitic. But to a Jew living here, or to one who only remembers the place with horror, such statements are little comfort among the flickering torches.[11]

The suggestion that Ukrainians might be genetically antisemitic, even within the syntactical context that suggests otherwise, is abhorrent, raising the specter of eugenic hatred and associating Ukrainians with Nazi ideology, reincarnated in "the flickering torches."

Stoking racial hatred, conjuring violence, asserting half-truths, and mistranslating source material marked this dismal failure to report on how Ukraine's leaders were attempting to forge a national identity while attempting to reconcile its past and improve conditions in the present. As Myron B. Kuropas of the American Ukrainian Justice Committee explained, "What some Jews did as agents of Soviet power to Ukrainians and others does not, of course, justify the negative perceptions or atrocious actions of some Ukrainians against Jews, but it does suggest that the latter's enmity was not simply the result of 'genetic anti-Semitism.'"[12] Kuropas's attempt to balance blame hints of a begrudging recognition. As one genocide scholar notes, "The members of a society can use resources from the collective memory in order to try to change the collective identity of their society, but changes to identity caused by changed conditions in society also influence what we choose to use from our collective memory."[13]

Despite the criticism leveled by political, religious, and educational leaders, CBS never offered to correct the factual errors or respond to a letter from Rabbi Yaakov Bleich, Chief Rabbi of Ukraine and one of the sources used in the segment, whose description of Ukrainian extremists, "'They're saying they want the Jews out. They want the Jews out, they want the Russians out, they want everybody out that's not an ethnic Ukrainian'"[14] was re-contextualized to suggest that these statements reflected the current Ukrainian government's policy or the attitude of the population at large. The failure to move discourse beyond the false equivalency of genocide comparisons stifles meaningful engagement.

Intellectual Pathology

This complicated period of time in Ukraine's history within a broader European history marking legitimated state terror against its own citizens and especially minorities – the very issue Jones raised time and again – generates questions about the purpose of scholarship: How do people move from strongly-held, competing, conflicting narratives of the past and reach some consensus that will be acceptable to all people of goodwill and bring about a degree of normalization in Ukrainian-Jewish relations? What constitutes consensus? What constitutes normalization? What discursive thread will allow a historiography in which representations are normalized to include both victimization and responsibility as perpetrators? The many historical and theoretical explanations for the genocides in Ukraine – whether within a generalized context or particularized dynamics behind the organization of pogroms in a specific locality – can be understood as a convergence of several contingencies, phenomena, and events. What we memorialize and how we commemorate events and historical figures become extensions of explainable phenomena.[15]

Jones has been, and likely will continue to be, branded as a Nazi sympathizer, in part, because immediately after his death in 1935 the Nazis appropriated his Soviet reporting, claiming him as their own in an obituary penned by Wiss. Another part of the narrative was quilted into a comfortable, homespun narrative of his undying loyalty to Germany, a beloved land that he had visited every year between 1923-1934. In that story, love of Germany becomes conflated with love of National Socialism. One must believe that Jones wrote the famine articles to assist Hitler's need to crush the communists and social democrats; to believe otherwise, one scholar asserted, is "simply naïve."[16] Jones showed Hitler to be a small but dangerous man, capable of untold misery, not unlike the portrait Dorothy Thompson offered in her 1932 feature for *Cosmopolitan*. Jones warned readers about Hitler's brutality towards the Jews and feared the worst was yet to come. In a revealing and symbolic act, Jones refused to give the Nazi salute at a Goering speech, his arm remaining "obstinately unraised."

Based on available documentation, that Jones had a deep, abiding love of Germany is obvious. However, to twist events of his life into a narrative in which his reporting of mass starvation is represented as collusion with the Nazi propaganda ministry is ultimately to deny the suffering of those Ukrainians who needlessly perished. Denial of the *Holodomor* can be seen as a form of "intellectual genocide by seeking to destroy the veracity of the memory of the survivors..." Genocide scholar Henry R. Huttenbach decries these attempts: "This, indeed, is a novel if not philosophically unique motivation, bordering on the intellectually pathological."[17]

If Jones is going to be represented as "Hero of Ukraine" in the service of validating the *Holodomor*, then that portrayal must be based on the discursive evidence he created. To accept his accounts of the *Holodomor* requires acknowledgment of Jones's work in full, not subjectively picking only those articles that show criticism of Soviet Bolshevism. For all his pointed criticisms of both Soviet and Nazi ideologies, Jones readily acknowledged and accounted for improvements that alleviated the effects of poverty and unemployment in measures taken by each dictatorship.

Jones's inclination to include multiple sides of a story should not be construed to mean he supported the regimes that he wrote about – favorably or unfavorably. Reducing his reporting to slogans and propaganda serves to manufacture consent and maintain the status quo that he felt compelled to question and attempted to better. Of course, the danger of mythologizing Gareth Jones by creating an impenetrable force field around him – perhaps dismissing flaws in his character and refusing to acknowledge errors in judgment and moral blind spots – undermines the need for open engagement with Jones's published and private communication. Jones continues to be used as political, cultural, and moral capital to advance ideological goals, which ultimately do not advance understanding of him. Coming to an understanding of Jones and the importance of his work requires further research, based more on responsible contextualization and less on reductive historiography.

Notes

1 Andrew Cairns, "Description of a Tour in the Volga Region," FO 371/16329, 169-193, in Tony Kuz, ed., *The Soviet Famine 1932-33: An Eye-Witness Account of Conditions in the Spring and Summer of 1932 by Andrew Cairns* (Edmonton, Alberta: Canadian Institute of Ukrainian Studies, 1989), 119-120.

2 Anatoly Podolsky, "Collaboration in Ukraine during the Holocaust: Aspects of Historiographyand Research," *The Holocaust in Ukraine: New Sources and Perspectives* (Washington, D.C.: US Holocaust Memorial Museum, 2013) 187-198.

3 "Mr Jones: anti-Soviet propaganda gets thumbs up from Ukrainian president." Accessed from https://thecommunists.org/2020/02/14/news/mr-jones-anti-soviet-propaganda-film-gets-thumbs-up-from-ukrainian-president-poroshenko/.

4 "Mr Jones: anti-Soviet propaganda."

5 Delmer, *Trail Sinister*, 142.

6 "Soviet Links Reich in Ukrainian Plot," *New York Times*, December 3, 1933, 26.

7 RGASPI, fond 81, list 3, file 99, sheets 146-151. See also Stalin and Kaganovich. *Correspondence 1931-1936* (Moscow, 2001).

8 Frank Sysyn, "The Ukrainian Famine of 1932-3: The Role of the Ukrainian Diaspora in Research and Public Discussion," in *Studies in Comparative Genocide*, eds. Levon Chorbajian and George Shirinian (New York: St. Martin's Press, 1999), 187.

9 Sysyn, "The Ukrainian Famine," 201.

10 Arthur Unger, "Stalinist 'famine' controversy. Film from '30s finally gets first US airing," *Christian Science Monitor*, September 24, 1986. Accessed from https://www.csmonitor.com/1986/0924/lvest-f.html.

11 Jeffrey Fager, prod., "The Ugly Face of Freedom," *60 Minutes*, October 23, 1994. Accessed from http://www.infoukes.com/politics/cbs60minutes/kuropas/.

12 Myron B. Kuropas, "Scourging a Nation: CBS and the Defamation of Ukraine," Ukrainian American Justice Committee (Kingston, Ontario: Kashtan Press, 1995). Accessed from http://www.infoukes.com/politics/cbs60minutes/kuropas/.

13 Barbar Törnquist-Plewa, "The Jedwabne Killings – A Challenge for Polish Collective Memory," in *Echoes of the Holocaust: Historical Cultures in Contemporary Europe*, eds. Klas-Göran Karlsson and Ulf Zander, 141-176, (Lund, Sweden: Nordic Academic Press, 2003), 168.

14 Quoted in Kuropas, "Scourging a Nation."

15 Wendy Lower, "Anti-Jewish Violence in Western Ukraine, Summer 1941: Varied Histories and Explanations," in *The Holocaust in Ukraine: New Sources and Perspectives* (Washington, D.C., Center for Advanced Holocaust Studies, United States Holocaust Memorial Museum, 2013), 143-177.

16 Teresa Charfas, "Teresa Cherfas responds," *Planet: The Welsh Internationalist*, 2013 (Summer 2013), 158.

17 Henry R. Huttenbach, "The Psychology and Politics of Genocide Denial: A Comparison of Four Case Studies," in *Studies in Comparative Genocide*, eds. Levon Chorbajian and George Shirinian, 216-229, (New York: St. Martin's Press, 1999), 221.

Index

Bibliography

NEWSPAPER ARTICLES

Jones, Gareth. "The Victim of 1930 – Familiar in Many Lands." *Western Mail*, December 31, 1930, 6.
— "Poland's Foreign Relations." *The Contemporary Review*, July 1931.
— "Fascist Dictatorship for Germany Now Possibility, Development." *New York American*, November 29, 1931.
— "A Retrospective of the Banking Crisis." *Western Mail*, December 21, 1931.
— "The Sphinx of German Politics." *Western Mail*, January 25, 1933.
— "Wales's Bonds with the Continent." *Western Mail*, February 7, 1933.
— "Germany Wants a New Frederick the Great." *Western Mail*, February 8, 1933.
— "Hitler Is There, But Will He Stay?" *Western Mail*, February 9, 1933.
— "German and Slav: Century Old Problems of Minorities." *Western Mail*, February 13, 1933.
— "The Ice Breaks in the Mountains." *Western Mail*, February 15, 1933.
— "Home Industries on their Death-Bed," *Western Mail*, February 17, 1933.
— "Workless Millions of German." *Western Mail*, February 21, 1933.
— "How Germany Tackles Unemployment." *Western Mail*, February 21, 1933.
— "Storm over the Polish Corridor." *Western Mail*, February 22, 1933.
— "The Red Light in East Europe." *Western Mail*, February 24, 1933.
— "With Hitler across Germany." *Western Mail*, February 28, 1933.
— "Beginning of German Fascism." *Western Mail*, March 1, 1933.
— "Primitive Worship of Hitler." *Western Mail*, March 2, 1933.
— "Whither Germany? Hitler Moving towards Dictatorship." *The Financial News*, March 1, 1933.
— "Whither Germany? The Clash between Industry and Agriculture." *The Financial News*, March 2, 1933.
— "Germany under the Rule of Hitler – Deathblow to Democracy." *Western Mail*, June 5, 1933.
— "Campaign of Hatred Against the Jews." *Western Mail*, June 7, 1933.
— "Germany Was Not Ready for Democracy." *Western Mail*, June 6, 1933.
— "Worship of the Soldier under the Nazi Regime." *Western Mail*, June 8, 1933.
— "Nazis' Interpretation of Christianity". *Western Mail*, June 9, 1933.
— "Methods of Nazis, Fascists and Bolsheviks." *Western Mail*, June 10, 1933.
— "How Germany Is Helping the Workless." *Western Mail*, April 27, 1933.
— "Social Service War on Unemployment." *Western Mail*, April 25, 1933.

— "Invisible Forces at the Conference." *Western Mail*, June 13, 1933.
— "Greater Tariffs – Chief Question at the World Conference." *Western Mail*, June 14, 1933.
— "Britain's Policy Before the World Conference." *Western Mail*, June 15, 1933.
— "The Nazi Tiger Claims New Prey," *Western Mail*, June 23, 1933, 8.
— "Storm over Europe," *Western Mail*, July 15, 1933, 9.
— "Herr Hitler's Breakaway – As the German Sees It," *Western Mail*, October 16, 1933, 11.
— "Hatchet Is Buried for Ten Years." *Western Mail*, January 29, 1934.
— "Origins of the National Eistedfodd." *Western Mail*, August 3, 1934.
— "The World's Perplexing Problems." *Western Mail*, May 9, 1934.
— "10,000 Planes on German Frontiers." *Western Mail*, June 29, 1934.
— "Fear of an Economic Storm in Germany." *Western Mail*, June 25, 1934.
— "Behind the Drama of Germany." *Western Mail*, July 2, 1934.
— "World Peace in Hands of Anglo-Saxons." *Western Mail*, June 27, 1934.
— "France Does Not Expect War at Present." *Western Mail*, August 3, 1934.
— "The Forces That Are Menacing Hitler." *Western Mail*, August 8, 1934.
— "Three Catastrophes in a Month." *Western Mail*, August 2, 1934.
— "Austria Torn by Dissension and Flaming with Hatred." *Western Mail* August 10, 1934.
— "Where War May Come From." *Western Mail*, August 15, 1934.
— "'Sacred Crusade' to Unite Austria with Germany." *Western Mail*, August 14, 1934.
— "Italy's Big Guns Point towards Austria." *Western Mail*, August 16, 1934.
— "The Hysteria of Goering." *Western Mail*, August 18, 1934.
— "Who Are the 'Yeses' and 'Noes' in the German Plebiscite?" *Western Mail*, August 21, 1934.
— "Hitler's Trump Card – Fear That Germany May Fall to Pieces." *Western Mail*, August 22, 1934.
— "Austrians 'Enslaved' by Italy." *Western Mail*, August 23, 1934.
— "A St. Bartholomew's Night on the Saar." *Western Mail*, October 25, 1934.
— "Will France Withhold Lorraine Iron Ore from the Saar?" *Western Mail*, October 26, 1934.
"Insist Hitler Act in Murder of Nazi." *New York Times*, December 31, 1932.
"Changed Policy of Hitler," *Western Mail*, January 16, 1934.
"Nazis Ruthless." *Western Mail*, July 10, 1934.
"Mr Gareth Jones." *Western Mail*, August 2, 1934.
"Soviet Links Reich in Ukrainian Plot." *New York Times*, December 3, 1933.
"German Journalist's Tribute to Audience." *Western Mail*, July 15, 1933.

LETTERS

Jones, Gareth. Letter dated July 15, 1923. Gareth Vaughan Jones Papers, National Library of Wales, File B6/1.

— Letter dated July 8, 1927. Gareth Vaughan Jones Papers, National Library of Wales, File B6/1.

— Letter dated August 16, 1927. Gareth Vaughan Jones Papers, National Library of Wales, File B6/1.

— Letter dated June 1928. Gareth Vaughan Jones Papers, National Library of Wales, File B6/1.

— Letter dated July 12, 1928. Gareth Vaughan Jones Papers, National Library of Wales, File B6/1.

— Letter dated July 18, 1928. Gareth Vaughan Jones Papers, National Library of Wales, File B6/1.

— Letter dated July 22, 1928. Gareth Vaughan Jones Papers, National Library of Wales, File B6/1.

— Letter dated August 1, 1928. Gareth Vaughan Jones Papers, National Library of Wales, File B6/1.

— Letter dated February 1929. Gareth Vaughan Jones Papers, National Library of Wales, File B6/2.

— Letter dated October 28, 1929. Gareth Vaughan Jones Papers, National Library of Wales, File B6/2.

— Letter dated August 26, 1930. Gareth Vaughan Jones Papers, National Library of Wales, Folder 16.

— Letter dated January 2, 1931. Gareth Vaughan Jones Papers, National Library of Wales, File B6/3.

— Letter dated October 27, 1931, Gareth Vaughan Jones Papers, National Library of Wales, Aberystwyth, File B6/3.

— Letter dated November 1931. Gareth Vaughan Jones Papers, National Library of Wales, File B6/3.

— Letter dated February 1932, Gareth Vaughan Jones Papers, National Library of Wales, File B6/4.

— Letter dated March 4, 1932, Gareth Vaughan Jones Papers, National Library of Wales, File B6/4.

— Letter dated April 17, 1932. Gareth Vaughan Jones Papers, National Library of Wales, File B6/3.

— Letter dated May 24, 1932, Gareth Vaughan Jones Papers, National Library of Wales, File B6/4.

— Letter dated July 11, 1932, Gareth Vaughan Jones Papers, National Library of Wales, Aberystwyth, File B6/4.

— Letter dated September 13, 1932, Gareth Vaughan Jones Papers, National Library of Wales, Aberystwyth, File B6/4.

— Letter dated September 14, 1932, Gareth Vaughan Jones Papers, National Library of Wales, Aberystwyth, File B6/4.

— Letter dated October 8, 1932, Gareth Vaughan Jones Papers, National Library of Wales, Aberystwyth, File B6/4.

— Letter dated October 25, 1932. Gareth Vaughan Jones Papers, National Library of Wales, Aberystwyth, File B6/4.

— Letter dated December 4, 1932, Gareth Vaughan Jones Papers, National Library of Wales, Aberystwyth, File B6/4.

— Letter dated December 21, 1932, Gareth Vaughan Jones Papers, National Library of Wales, File B6/5.

— Letter dated, January 6, 1933, Gareth Vaughan Jones Papers, National Library of Wales, File 14.

— Letter dated Wednesday, January 18, 1933, Gareth Vaughan Jones Papers, National Library of Wales, File B6/5.

— Letter dated Thursday, January 19, 1933, Gareth Vaughan Jones Papers, National Library of Wales, File 14.

— Letter dated Wednesday, January 18, 1933, Gareth Vaughan Jones Papers, National Library of Wales, File 14.

— Letter dated Friday, January 20, 1933, Gareth Vaughan Jones Papers, National Library of Wales, File 14.

— Letter dated January 23, 1933, Gareth Vaughan Jones Papers, National Library of Wales, File 14.

— Letter dated January 25, 1933, Gareth Vaughan Jones Papers, National Library of Wales, File B6/5.

— Letter dated January 27, 1933, Gareth Vaughan Jones Papers, National Library of Wales, File B6/5.

— Letter dated Sunday, January 29, 1933, Gareth Vaughan Jones Papers, National Library of Wales, File 14.

— Letter dated February 5, 1933, Gareth Vaughan Jones Papers, National Library of Wales, Aberystwyth, File 14.

— Letter dated February 9, 1933, Gareth Vaughan Jones Papers, National Library of Wales, File 14.

— Letter dated February 12, 1933, Gareth Vaughan Jones Papers, National Library of Wales, Aberystwyth, File B6/4.

— Letter dated February 19, 1933. Gareth Vaughan Jones Papers, National Library of Wales, Aberystwyth, File 14.

— Letter dated February 26, 1933. Gareth Vaughan Jones Papers, National Library of Wales, Aberystwyth, File 14.

— Letter dated March 1, 1933, Gareth Vaughan Jones Papers, National Library of Wales, Aberystwyth, File 14.

— Letter dated March 14, 1933, Gareth Vaughan Jones Papers, National Library of Wales, Aberystwyth, File 14.

— Letter dated March 27, 1933, Gareth Vaughan Jones Papers, National Library of Wales Library, Aberystwyth, File B6/5.

— Letter dated March 31, 1933. Gareth Vaughan Jones Papers, National Library of Wales, Aberystwyth, File 14.

— Letter dated May 3, 1933, Gareth Vaughan Jones Papers, National Library of Wales Library, Aberystwyth, File B6/5.

— "The Peasants in Russia – Exhausted Supplies." *Manchester Guardian*, May 8, 1933. Accessed from https://www.garethjones.org/soviet_articles/peasants_in_russia.htm.

— Letter to the Editor – Mr. Jones Replies, *New York Times*, May 13, 1933.

— To the Editor of *The Welshman*, September 16, 1933.

— Letter dated May 12, 1933. Gareth Vaughan Jones Papers, National Library of Wales, File B6/5.

— Letter dated May 28, 1933. Gareth Vaughan Jones Papers, National Library of Wales, Aberystwyth, File B6/5.

— Letter dated June 11, 1933, Gareth Vaughan Jones Papers, National Library of Wales Library, Aberystwyth, File B6/5.

— Letter date June 18, 1933. Gareth Vaughan Jones Papers, National Library of Wales, File B6/5.

— Letter dated May 11, 1934. Gareth Vaughan Jones Papers, National Library of Wales, Aberystwyth, File B 6/5.

— Letter dated June 10, 1934. Gareth Vaughan Jones Papers, National Library of Wales, Aberystwyth, File B6/5.

— Letter dated July 16, 1934. Gareth Vaughan Jones Papers, National Library of Wales, Aberystwyth, File B6/5.

— Letters dated July 26, 29, 31, August 1, 1934. Gareth Vaughan Jones Papers, National Library of Wales, Aberystwyth, File B6/5.

— Letter dated August 3, 1934. Gareth Vaughan Jones Papers, National Library of Wales, Aberystwyth, File B6/5.

— Letter dated August 5, 1934. Gareth Vaughan Jones Papers, National Library of Wales, Aberystwyth, File B6/5.

— Letter dated August 13, 1934, Gareth Vaughan Jones Papers, National Library of Wales, Aberystwyth, File B6/5.

— Letter dated August 19, 1934, Gareth Vaughan Jones Papers, National Library of Wales, Aberystwyth, File B6/5.

von Dirksen, Herbert. Letter dated June 16, 1933.

Gill, H. C. "Position of Minority Races in Czechoslovakia" [Letter to the Editor]. *Western Mail*, February 23, 1933.

Muggeridge, Malcolm. Letter dated September 29, 1933. Gareth Vaughan Jones Papers, National Library of Wales, Aberystwyth, File B6/7.

NOTEBOOK and APPOINTMENT DIARIES

Jones, Gareth. Diary – Europe and Russia, 1931, Gareth Vaughan Jones Papers, National Library of Wales, File B1/6.

— Appointment and Engagement Diary 1932, Gareth Vaughan Jones Papers, National Library of Wales, Aberystwyth, File B1/8.

— Journal of a Tour of Germany, 1933, Gareth Vaughan Jones Papers, National Library of Wales, Aberystwyth, File B1/14.

— Hitler Diary, 1933, Gareth Vaughan Jones Papers, National Library of Wales, Aberystwyth, File B1/9.
— Impressions of Germany Diary, December 1932, Gareth Vaughan Jones Papers, National Library of Wales, Aberystwyth, File B3/12.
— Russian Notes, 1933, Gareth Vaughan Jones Papers, National Library of Wales, Aberystwyth, File B3/14.
— Journal of a Tour of Germany, 1933, Gareth Vaughan Jones Papers, National Library of Wales, File B1/14.
— Diary of Tour of Russia, 1933, Diary 3. Gareth Vaughan Jones Papers, National Library of Wales, Aberystwyth, File B1/16.
— Trieste Diary [Notebook], August 1934, Gareth Vaughan Jones Papers, National Library of Wales, Aberystwyth, File 41.
— Travels in Germany, [June] 1934, Gareth Vaughan Jones Papers, National Library of Wales, Aberystwyth, File B3/17.
— Tour of Central Europe 1934, Gareth Vaughan Jones Pagers, National Library of Wales, Aberystwyth, File B3/15.
— Travels in the United States, Gareth Vaughan Jones Papers, National Library of Wales, Aberystwyth, File B3/16.
— Diary of a Trip to Germany, 1934, Gareth Vaughan Jones Papers, National Library of Wales, Aberystwyth, File 42.

MISCELLANEOUS

Jones, Gareth. "Impressions of Germany." Memorandum, December 1932. Accessed from https://www.garethjones.org/german_articles/impressions1932.htm.
— Lecture titled "Soviet Russia in March 1933," Royal Institute of International Affairs, 30 March 1933. Gareth Vaughan Jones Papers, National Library of Wales, Aberystwyth, File A/4.
Biography of Reinhard Haferkorn, accessed from http://discovery.nationalarchives.gov.uk/SearchUI/details?Uri=C11050176.
Cairns, Andrew. "Description of a Tour in the Volga Region." FO 371/16329, 169-193, in Tony Kuz, ed. *The Soviet Famine 1932-33: An Eye-Witness Account of Conditions in the Spring and Summer of 1932 by Andrew Cairns*. Edmonton, Alberta: Canadian Institute of Ukrainian Studies, 1989.
Fager, Jeffrey, prod. "The Ugly Face of Freedom," *60 Minutes*, October 23, 1994. Accessed from http://www.infoukes.com/politics/cbs60minutes/kuropas/.
Fröhlich, Elke (ed.). *Die Tagebücher von Joseph Goebbels, Teil I* Register 1923–1941. [The Diaries of Joseph Goebbels,Volume 2/ Part III: Register, 1923-1941]. Accessed from https://www.garethjones.org/goebbels2/goebbels.htm.
Heinz, Jr., H. J. *Experiences in Russia 1931 – A Diary*. Pittsburgh, Pennsylvania: Alton Press, 1932.
Kuropas, Myron B. "Scourging a Nation: CBS and the Defamation of Ukraine." Ukrainian American Justice Committee. Kingston, Ontario: Kashtan Press,

1995. Accessed from http://www.infoukes.com/politics/cbs60minutes/kuropas/.

Lee, Ivy. "Publication on War Debts & Gold Crisis." Address delivered at DePauw University, Greencastle, Indiana, February 21, 1932, n.p. Accessed from https://www.garethjones.org/american_articles/ivy_lee.htm.

Press Release. *Brüder in Not*. Accessed from https://www.garethjones.org/soviet_articles/bruder_in_not_1.htm.

SECONDARY SOURCES

Arendt, Hannah. *The Origins of Totalitarianism*. New York: The World Publishing Company, 1958.

Boveri, Margaret. *Wür lügen alle*. Berlin: Olten and Freiburg, 1965.

Carvalho, Anabela. "Media(ted) Discourse and Society." *Journalism Studies*, 2008, 9(2), 161-177.

Carynnyk, Marco. "'A Knife in the Back of Our Revolution': A Reply to Alexander J. Motyl's 'The Ukrainian Nationalist Movement and the Jews: Theoretical Reflections on Nationalism, Fascism, Rationality, Primordialism, and History.'" Accessed from https://www.academia.edu/6313351/A_Knife_in_the_Back_of_Our_Revolution_A_Reply_to_Alexander_J_Motyls_The_Ukrainian_Nationalist_Movement_and_the_Jews_Theoretical_Reflections_on_Nationalism_Fascism_Rationality_Primordialism_and_History.

Carynnyk, Marco, Luciuk, Lubomyr Y., and Kordan, Bohdan S., eds., *The Foreign Office and the Great Famine of 1932-1933*. Kingston Ontario: The Limestone Press, 1988.

Cesarani, David. "The London *Jewish Chronicle* and the Holocaust." In Robert Moses Shapiro, ed., *Why Didn't the Press Shout? American & International Journalism During the Holocaust*, 175-196. Jersey City, New Jersey: Yeshiva University Press, 2003.

Cherfas, Therasa. "'Germany, my Beloved Land' Gareth Jones and the Nazis." *Planet: The Welsh Internationalist*, 210 (Summer 2013), 66-77.

— "Teresa Cherfas responds." *Planet: The Welsh Internationalist*, 2013 (Summer 2013), 157-158.

Colley, Dr. Margaret Siriol. *More Than a Grain of Truth: The Biography of Gareth Richard Vaughan Jones*. Newark, Nottinghamshire, 2005.

Davies, Geraint Talfan. The Girl in the Diary. BBC One, Wales. 12 August 2014. Accessed English transcript from https://subsaga.com/bbc/entertainment/gohebwyr/cyfres-1/geraint-talfan-davies.html.

Delmer, Sefton. *Trail Sinister: An* Autobiography. London: Secker and Warburg, 1961.

Dietrich, Kris. *Taboo Genocide: 1933 & the Extermination of Ukraine – Volume II*. Xlibris, 2015.

Gamache, Ray. "Breaking Eggs for a Holodomor: Walter Duranty, the *New York Times*, and the Denigration of Gareth Jones." *Journalism History*, 39:4 (Winter 2014), 208-218.

— "Contextualizing FDR's Campaign to Recognize the Soviet Union, 1932-1933: Propaganda, Genocide Denial, and Ukrainian Resistance," *Harvard Ukrainian Studies Journal*, 37(2), [pre-print].

— *Gareth Jones: Eyewitness to the Holodomor*. Cardiff, Wales: Welsh Academic Press, 2012.

Grossberg, Lawrence. "Reality Is Bad Enough, Draft Chapter One." Accessed from https://www.researchgate.net/publication/321805684_REALITY _IS_BAD_ENOUGH_DRAFT_CHAPTER_ONE?channel=doi&linkId=5a 32a57b0f7e9b2a287c1c41&showFulltext=true.

Haferkorn, Reinhard. "Danzig and the Polish Corridor." *International Affairs* (Royal Institute of International Affairs 1931-1939) 12, no. 2 (1933): 224-239. Accessed 14 July 2020, doi:10.2307/2602567.

Hiebert, Ray Eldon. *Courtier to the Crowd: Ivy Lee and the Development of Public Relations in America*. New York: PR Museum Press, 2017.

Hobusch, Harald. "Rescuing German Alpine Tradition: Nanga Parbat and Its Visual Afterlife." *Journal of Sport History*, Vol. 29.1 (Summer 2002), 49-76.

Huttenbach, Henry H. "The Psychology and Politics of Genocide Denial: A Comparison of Four Case Studies." in *Studies in Comparative Genocide*, eds. Levon Chorbajian and George Shirinian, 216-229. New York: St. Martin's Press, 1999.

Leff, Laural. "When the Facts Didn't Speak for Themselves: The Holocaust and the *New York Times*, 1939-1945." In Robert Moses Shapiro, ed., *Why Didn't the Press Shout? American & International Journalism During the Holocaust*, 51-78. Jersey City, New Jersey: Yeshiva University Press, 2003.

Lipstadt, Deborah E. *Beyond Belief: The American Press & the Coming of the Holocaust 1933-1945*. New York: The Free Press, 1986.

Lochner, Louis P. *What About Germany?* New York: Dodd, Mead & Company, 1942.

Lower, Wendy. "Anti-Jewish Violence in Western Ukraine, Summer 1941: Varied Histories and Explanations," in *The Holocaust in Ukraine: New Sources and Perspectives*, 143-177. Washington, D.C., Center for Advanced Holocaust Studies, United States Holocaust Memorial Museum, 2013.

Lyons, Eugene. *Assignment in Utopia*. New York: Harcourt, Brace and Company, 1937.

Podolsky, Anatoly. "Collaboration in Ukraine during the Holocaust: Aspects of Historiography and Research." *The Holocaust in Ukraine: New Sources and Perspectives*. Washington, D.C.: US Holocaust Memorial Museum, 2013, 187-198.

Regnery, Henry. *Perfect Sowing: Reflections of a Bookman*. Wilmington, Del.: ISI Books, 1999.

Schneidermann, Daniel. *Berlin, 1933: La presse internationale face à Hitler*. Paris: Éditions du Seuil, 2018.

Skinner, Robert. Notes on a Conversation with Professor Samuel N. Harper. Despatch No. 871, October 27, 1932. State Department Archives, Living Conditions/550/861.5017. Accessed from https://www.fold3/image/68313029.

Snyder, Timothy. *Bloodlands – Europe between Hitler and Stalin.* New York: Basic Books, 2017.

Stewart, Frida. *Firing a Shot for Freedom: The Memoirs of Frida Stewart.* London: The Clapton Press, 2020.

Sysyn, Frank. "The Ukrainian Famine of 1932-3: The Role of the Ukrainian Diaspora in Research and Public Discussion." in *Studies in Comparative Genocide,* eds. Levon Chorbajian and George Shirinian, 182-215. New York: St. Martin's Press, 1999.

Tornquist-Plewa, Barbar. "The Jedwabne Killings – A Challenge for Polish Collective Memory." in *Echoes of the Holocaust: Historical Cultures in Contemporary Europe,* eds. Klas-Göran Karlsson and Ulf Zander, 141-176. Lund, Sweden: Nordic Academic Press, 2003.

Unger, Arthur. "Stalinist 'famine' controversy. Film from '30s finally gets first US airing," *Christian Science Monitor,* September 24, 1986. Accessed from https://www.csmonitor.com/1986/0924/lvest-f.html.

Vossler, Ronald J., ed. *We'll Meet Again in Heaven: Germans in the Soviet Union Write Their American Relatives (1925-1937),* trans. Ronald J. Vossler. Fargo, North Dakota: Germans from Russia Heritage Collection, 2001.

Wainewright, Will. *Reporting on Hitler.* London: Biteback Press, 2017.

welsh academic press

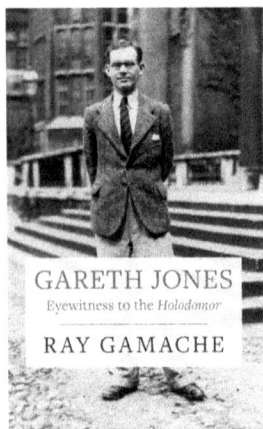

GARETH JONES
Eyewitness to the Holodomor

Ray Gamache

'*Excellent ... serves as a warning to journalists not to be taken in by official sources and political ideology but to report what they actually learn through their own efforts.*'
Prof. Maurine H. Beasley, Univ. of Maryland

'*...meticulously researched book [that] returns Gareth Jones to his rightful status, as one of the most outstanding journalists of his generation*'
Nigel Linsan Colley, www.garethjones.org

'*Extraordinary ... Jones' articles ... caused a sensation ... Because [his] notebooks record immediate impressions and describe events as they were happening, they have an unusual freshness ... Jones' reputation has revived thanks to the Ukrainian government's broader efforts to tell the history of the famine.*'
Anne Applebaum, The New York Review

Gareth Jones (1905-1934), the young Welsh investigative journalist, is revered in Ukraine as a national hero and is now rightly recognised as the first reporter to reveal the horror of the Holodomor, the Soviet Government-induced famine of the early 1930s, which killed millions of Ukrainians.

978-1-86057-1220	256pp	£19.99	PB
978-1-86057-1466	256pp	£19.99	EBK

MR JONES
The Man Who Knew Too Much
The Life and Death of Gareth Jones

Martin Shipton

'*Martin Shipton's biography is a much needed and welcome contribution to our understanding of Jones' experiences and his life*'
Mick Antoniw MS

Murdered in Mongolia in 1935 aged only 29, Gareth Jones is a national hero in Ukraine for being the first reporter to reveal the truth about the Holodomor – the 1932-33 genocide inflicted on Ukraine by the Soviet Union during which over four million people perished.

Drawing upon Jones' articles, notebooks and private correspondence, Martin Shipton, the highly respected political journalist at Jones' former   newspaper, the Western Mail, reveals the remarkable yet tragically short life of this fascinating and determined Welshman who pioneered the role of investigative journalism.

978-1-86057-1435	374pp (inc. 82 images)	£19.99	PB
978-1-86057-1565	374pp (inc. 82 images)	£19.99	EBK

welsh academic press

MORGAN JONES
Man of Conscience

Wayne David

'*Wayne David deserves great credit for bringing Morgan Jones to life in this well-researched and very readable book.*'
Nick Thomas-Symonds MP

'*Wayne David writes of one of his predecessors as Labour MP for Caerphilly with the understanding of the political insider and the contextual knowledge of the historian.*'
Professor Dai Smith

'*Jones was a man of principle and pragmatism.*'
Hilary Benn MP, from his Foreword

Imprisoned in Wormwood Scrubs for his pacifist beliefs during the First World War, Morgan Jones made history by becoming the first conscientious objector to be elected an MP when he won the Caerphilly by-election for Labour in 1921.

978-1-86057-1411	128pp	£16.99	PB
978-1-86057-1541	128pp	£16.99	EBK

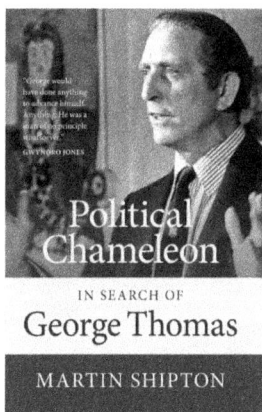

POLITICAL CHAMELEON
In Search of George Thomas

Martin Shipton

'*Compelling*'
Kevin McGuire

'*A brilliant book*'
Guto Harri

'*I picked up this book expecting it to be a hatchet job, but it is a very fair book and a very well researched book. The problem with George Thomas is that one can write a book that is very fair and very well researched yet he still comes out of it very badly.*'
Vaughan Roderick, BBC Radio Wales

Drawing on previously unpublished material from Thomas' vast personal and political archive in the National Library of Wales, and interviews with many who knew him during his career, award-winning journalist Martin Shipton reveals the real George Thomas, the complex character behind the carefully crafted facade of the devout Christian, and discovers a number of surprising and shocking personae – including the sexual predator – of this ultimate *Political Chameleon*.

978-1-86057-137-4	304pp	£16.99	PB

welsh academic press

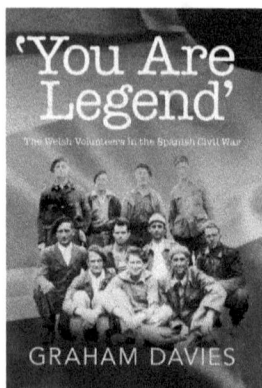

'YOU ARE LEGEND'
The Welsh Volunteers in the Spanish Civil War

Graham Davies

'Excellent. A paean to the working men and women of Wales who went to Spain to fight in defence of the fledgling Spanish Republic.'
Keith Jones, son of volunteer Tom Jones from Rhosllanerchrugog

'Well researched, and using previously unpublished sources, 'You Are Legend' is recommended reading. It is important that the contribution of the large number of Welsh volunteers continues to be recognised.'
Mary Greening, daughter of volunteer Edwin Greening of Aberdare

'A highly readable and comprehensively researched account of the Welsh Brigaders.'
Alan Warren, Spanish Civil War historian

Almost 200 Welshmen and women volunteered to join the International Brigade and travelled to Spain to fight fascism alongside the Republican government during the 1936-1939 Spanish Civil War. While over 150 returned home, at least 35 died during the brutal conflict. *'You Are Legend'* is their remarkable story.

978-1-86057-1305	224pp	£19.99	PB
978-1-86057-1558	224pp	£19.99	EBK

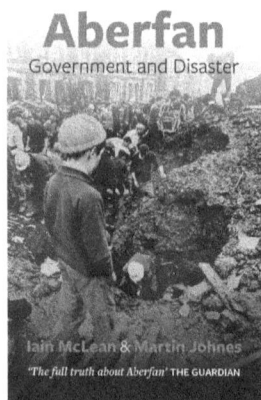

ABERFAN
Government and Disaster
(Second Edition)

Iain McLean & Martin Johnes

'The full truth about Aberfan'
The Guardian

'The research is outstanding...the investigation is substantial, balanced and authoritative...this is certainly the definitive book on the subject...Meticulous.'
John R. Davis, Journal of Contemporary British History

'Excellent...thorough and sympathetic.'
Headway 2000 (Aberfan Community Newspaper)

'Intelligent and moving'
Planet

Aberfan - Government & Disaster is widely recognised as the definitive study of the disaster and, following meticulous research of previously unavailable public records - kept confidential by the UK Government's 30-year rule - the authors explain how and why the disaster happened and why nobody was held responsible.

978-1-86057-1336	224pp (+16pp photo section)	£19.99	PB
978-1-86057-1459	224pp (+16pp photo section)	£19.99	EBK

www.ingramcontent.com/pod-product-compliance
Lightning Source LLC
Chambersburg PA
CBHW071124280326
41935CB00010B/1109